*Jayne Persico presents...*

# Glass Kiln Casting with Colour de Verre

Wardell
PUBLICATIONS INC

**Jayne Persico presents...**
**Glass Kiln Casting with Colour de Verre**
**is Copyright© 2007 by**
**Wardell Publications Inc.**

**All Designs, Drawings and Images are**
**Copyright© 2007 by Jayne Persico**

**Cataloging in Publication Data**

Persico, Jayne

Jayne Persico presents... Glass Kiln Casting with Colour de Verre / Jayne Persico; text editor, Randy Wardell; jewelry design & fabrication, Jayne Persico; photography, Mark Bailey.

Includes index

ISBN-13: 978-0-919985-55-1

ISBN-10: 0-919985-55-6

1. Glass fusing. I. Wardell, Randy A. (Randy Allan), 1954- II. Title. III. Title: Glass Kiln Casting with Colour de Verre.

NK5440.J48P473 2007 748.2'028 C2007-904816-6

Printed in Thailand by Phongwarin Printing Ltd.
Published simultaneously in Canada and USA
E-mail: info@wardellpublications.com
Website: www.wardellpublications.com

*Jayne Persico presents...*

# Glass Kiln Casting with Colour de Verre


*Author*
Jayne Persico

*Editor*
Randy Wardell

*Glass Design & Fabrication*
Jayne Persico

*Photography*
Mark Bailey

*Book Layout & Typography*
Randy Wardell



*Acknowledgements*

My deepest appreciation to Dody Ottaviani, Craig Smith, & Larry Jacobsen, for their wonderful assistance, both in the studio and in the classroom but most especially for being wonderful friends. Thanks and appreciation to Randy Wardell, my editor & publisher and also to my photographer Mark Bailey. I truly value the support from The Uroboros Glass Studios, Coatings by Sandberg, Spectrum Glass Co., Aim Kilns, Skutt Kilns, Gemini Saw Co. and The Glastar Corporation. And finally an extraordinary thank-you to my family for their love and support!

*Published by*

To receive our electronic newsletter or to send suggestions please contact us
by E-mail: info@wardellpublications.com or visit our Website: www.wardellpublications.com

## A Message from the Author

I have to admit, when I first started working with frit I was not all that pleased with the results. But I was so drawn to Pâte de Verre casting (French for 'Paste of Glass') that I was determined to learn everything I could about frit. As luck would have it, I came across a wonderful opportunity to study with Kimiake and Shinichi Higuchi at The Studio of The Corning Museum of Glass, and that was exactly what I needed. Kimiake and Shinichi Higuchi are world-renowned masters of Pâte de Verre. Their art pieces have won many international awards and are included in many significant glass collections such as the Corning Museum of Glass and the Kitazawa Museum of Art. My time with Kimiake and Shinichi was well spent as I gained a new respect for frit and my work improved immediately. Three of the objects I created in this workshop are shown on this page.

*Pâte de Verre 'Pansies' created by the author at The Studio of The Corning Museum of Glass, under the direction of Kimiake and Shinichi Higuchi.*

I have been casting glass for many years using traditional techniques including the complex but rewarding 'lost wax' process to create glass sculptures. However my favorite technique is 'component casting,' when several design elements (components) are assembled in some way to make one complete sculptural object. This 'assembly' can be accomplished in two ways. One method involves the creation of a series of flexible silicone components that are mounted onto a clay base then a refractory mold is created from this design to use for glass casting. The other method - the one I will expand on in this book - involves casting each glass component individually then attach them to a base of glass by tack fusing in the kiln. I call my style of component casting 'Glass Kiln Casting' where I use commercially available molds created specifically for this purpose by 'Colour de Verre.'

*'Floral Vessel #1' created by the author at The Studio of The Corning Museum of Glass*

When Craig Smith & I formed Colour de Verre (see page 6 & 7 for the 'Colour de Verre' story) I knew immediately that this incredible format of reusable casting molds would be an excellent introduction to Glass Kiln Casting for all glass artists. I am delighted to share my expertise with you in this book, to enable all glass artists to benefit from Glass Kiln Casting with Colour de Verre molds.

*Jayne Persico*

## Author Contact Information

J. P. Glassworks Studio

50 North Vine Street,

Hazleton, PA 18201 USA

Email: info@jpglassworks.com

Website: www.jpglassworks.com

*Kiln Formed Bracelet by the author, executed in the Pâte de Verre method under the direction of Kimiake and Shinichi Higuchi.*

## *Table Of Contents*



## *Glass Kiln Casting - Showcase Galleries*

*'Positive Energy Waves' by the author using the Glass Damming technique shown in chapter 9 on pages 60 - 63.*

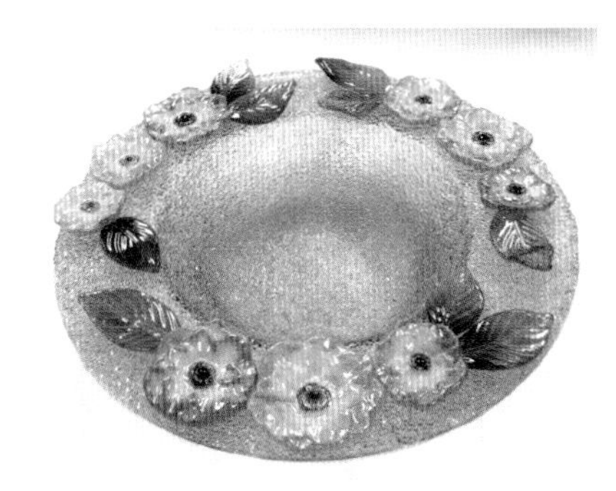

*'Bowl with Flower Rim' by the author, accomplish using the 'Multiple Component' casting technique covered in chapter 6 on pages 38 - 41.*

# Chapter 1 - An Introduction to Glass Frit Casting

Glass Frit Casting is not exactly new. In fact a similar process called Pâte de Verre (French for 'Paste of Glass') has been around for thousands of years. Some of the techniques in this book are new but the most important new development is the ceramic casting molds that have enabled us to create glass art in ways that were either difficult to achieve (i.e. using one-off molds) or totally unavailable to the average glass artisan.

This first chapter provides background into the 'Colour de Verre' molds. Plus it has important information on the Preparation and Care of the molds (pg 8), a review of the Tools, Materials & Equipment (pg 10), and an uncloaking of the mysteries behind the Digital Kiln Controller (pg 12). So what are you waiting for - let's do some 'Glass Kiln Casting'!

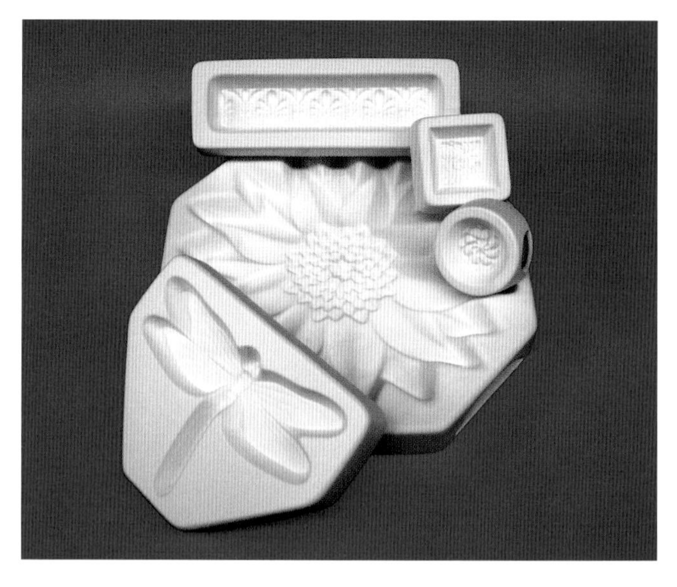

*A selection of the 'Glass Frit Casting' molds that we will be using to create the projects presented in this book.*

## *The 'Colour de Verre' Molds Story*

by Craig Smith - mold maker

Jayne and I met in 2003. It was an early spring evening and she had just finished teaching a class in kiln casting. I had been working all day in my studio. I had only been out once that day - to run down to the store, catch lunch, and pick up some wine and snacks to offer my guests.

A mutual friend had arranged to meet Jayne after her class and together they would swing by my house and studio. It would be our opportunity to meet and my opportunity to show Jayne the mold technology and product prototypes I had developed.

Let me give you some background. I am a classically trained traditional ceramicist. I designed and created functional and decorative pieces that I sold at craft shows, in galleries, and through high-end department stores. Around 1990 I realized that the mold-making skills I had developed in order to execute my own work were in high demand. My career and business transitioned to working with artists and companies to creating molds and mold systems based on their work and designs. My molds permitted them to generate artwork and products in a more economical and efficient manner.

So, back to Jayne. She arrived at my house and, since the evening had turned too cool for us to sit outside, we sat around my dinning room table snacking on black, salt-cured olives and sipping wine. Sitting in the middle of the table was one of my first frit mold prototypes; a dragonfly. I explained how the mold was reusable; how its' design permitted uniform heating and cooling; and how it could be mass-produced without sacrificing quality, design or detail.

Jayne was very excited. She said that she had produced one-off Hydroperm® and silica molds for her own artwork. She knew her students were very interested in learning this process so they could create complex designs in glass. However, she discovered that students were often overwhelmed and intimidated by the mold making process.

While I knew a bit about the mechanics of glass from my ceramics background, I freely admitted that I knew little - actually nothing - about introducing glass artists to this new technology. Additionally, I knew Jayne's teaching and market experience would be invaluable in choosing designs and formats that would appeal to the rapidly growing art glass market. So, there, in our dinning room, we toasted to the formation of our new company, Colour de Verre.

I am often asked how a new mold design is created. Well, there are about six steps in the progression to the final product. It starts with an actual size model of what the final glass piece is to look like. This form is sculpted either by Jayne or myself or sometimes as a collaboration between the two of us. When we are satisfied with the prototype sculpture, I carefully refine it then add a 'collection reservoir' to the backside. This model is encased in a high-tech plaster. After it has hardened it is trimmed, carved and refined again. After much work the model mold should look just like the Colour de Verre product that it will become - except it is solid. This is called the 'master model.' I won't bore you with all the details but there are three more steps before the final production 'investment' mold is ready.

These production molds are made from a soft, porous plaster designed to absorb water. The molds are filled with liquid clay that is specially formulated for Colour de Verre molds, designed to withstand thermal stresses. The water content of the liquid clay will be absorbed by the soft production mold, leaving behind a hollow shell. This hollow shell is extracted, cleaned and fired to become the typical hard shell Colour de Verre mold that you can buy and use.

*The Colour de Verre 'Pendant Mold' at the top was used to cast the glass cabochon mounted in this sterling silver pendant frame. This mold is featured in the second half of chapter 11 on page 72*

So, why do we go to all this trouble to make the Colour de Verre molds hollow? It is all about heat transfer. Solid form molds generally have thick and thin sections that heat unevenly. The thicker areas will slow the heat transfer to the glass while the thinner areas will heat more quickly. In addition the top surface of the glass would heat much more rapidly than the bottom surface particularly those areas in contact with the dense, solid mold. As any aspiring glass artist knows, stable, consistent heating and cooling is essential to avoid unwanted breaking and cracking.

Jayne is my friend, but I truly believe that I am being impartial when I tell you that she is a wonderful teacher. This book will provide a guide to help you create some spectacular pieces and it will inspire you to develop new and interesting techniques of your own.

*The mold above is one of several Colour de Verre 'Bracelet' molds that can be used to cast a glass blank to create a kiln formed bracelet.*

*The 'Kiln Formed' bracelets above were cast in the mold shown at left then formed on a bracelet mandrel. See chapter 12 on page 74 for details on how it's done.*

# Molds: Preparation, Care and Firing

Molds for casting glass seem almost magical. They present an opportunity to fusers to create three-dimensional objects, with textures and shapes that would be otherwise unavailable through kiln working alone. When casting molds are united with glass frits the possibilities are almost endless and always exciting. Add the creative energy of an artist's eye and the magic is set in motion. However, this chapter is not about the creative process - it's about the stewardship of these wonderful tools. It is essential for us to prepare them for their job then take proper care of them, to preserve them, so they can take care of our work.

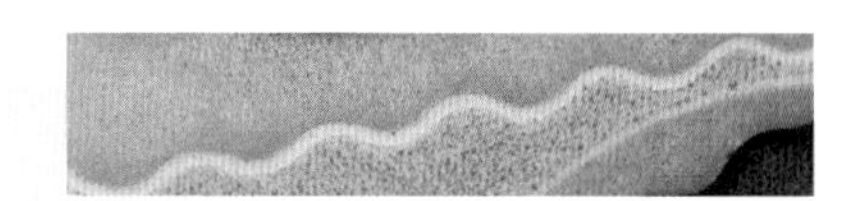

***Tools & Equipment:***

- ***Mold Preparation:*** Primo Primer™, applicator brush (soft, round), hairdryer
- ***Safety:*** Dust mask, safety glasses, kiln gloves

***Forming Mold:***

- 'Colour de Verre' - all shapes and designs

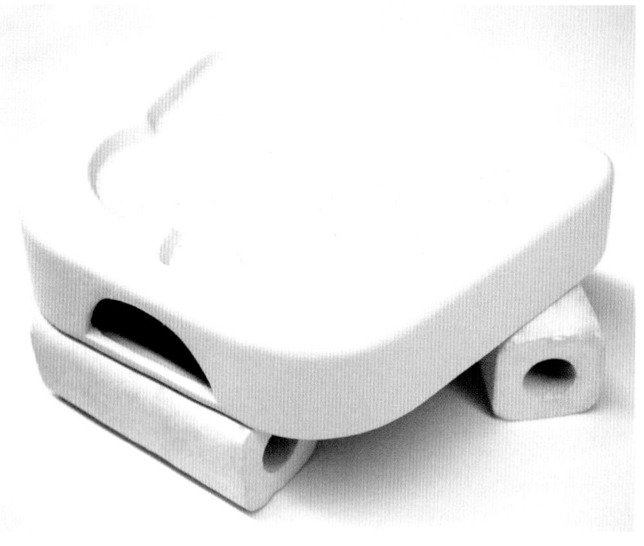

## *Why Primo Primer™?*

We recommend using Hotline Primo Primer™ on all Colour de Verre molds. We've tested the complete assortment of kiln washes and primers available on the market as of this writing. Only Hotline Primo Primer™ consistently delivered all three properties that we feel are essential for mold casting.

- Permits thin, even coats that won't fill in and cover up design details
- Consistent and reliable glass release
- Can be easily removed after firing

**1.** Mix by volume one part Hotline Primo Primer™ to five parts water. Keep the primer well stirred. The primer's fine particles, the active components, will settle out of the mixture rapidly and start to cake on the container's bottom. Get into the habit of using your applicator brush to stir these particles off the bottom of the container and back into the solution.

**2.** Use a soft round brush to apply primer to the mold's inside surface and topside. Dry the primer with a handheld hair dryer between each coat and again after the final coat. You can tell the primer is dry when it becomes lighter in color. Apply a total of four to five thin coats of primer on a new mold. A mold that has been previously fired only needs three thin coats of primer (after being cleaned).

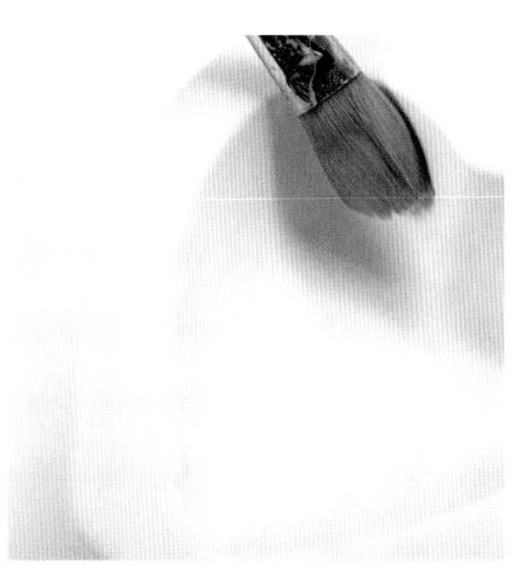
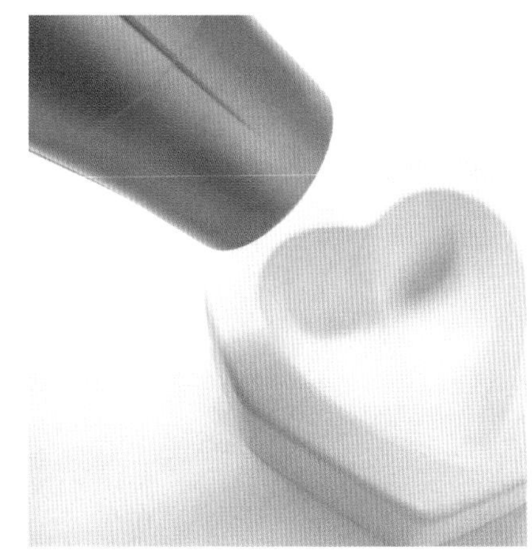

## *Firing Colour de Verre Molds:*

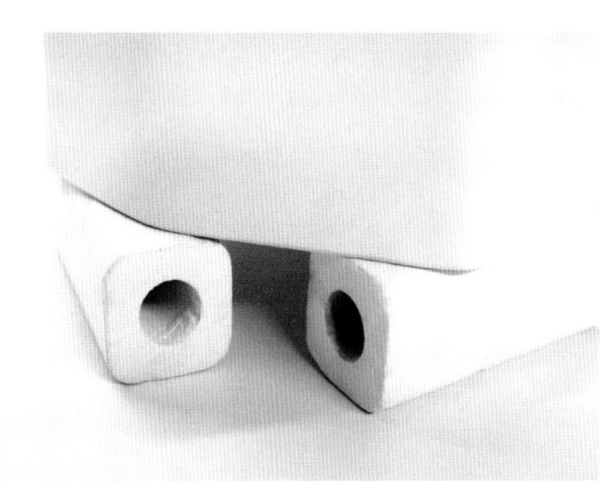

3. Color de Verre molds are hollow, designed with an 'open face' format. This unique design allows the heat to circulate more easily. You will notice that the firing schedules in this book are a bit lower in temperature and have a shorter soak time than the firing schedules for solid mold casting. These firing schedules are only for Colour de Verre molds using the frit size specified in each chapter. Since every kiln can vary slightly in firing temperatures I strongly recommend test firing small frit projects to determine what the correct temperature will be for your kiln. (See more on this in the Digital Controller section on page 12).
4. Promote air circulation under the mold by elevating it on kiln posts when firing. Simply lay three kiln posts on their side on the kiln shelf then carefully position the filled mold on these posts. Make sure the mold is level and stable. I like to keep a small level near my kiln to check the mold before closing the lid.
5. After each firing the mold must be cleaned to remove all traces of the old primer. There are two ways to clean the mold, wet or dry. When cleaning it dry you absolutely must wear a dust mask. Remove the primer with a stiff brush in a well-ventilated area or outside. When all the old primer is removed the mold is ready to be recoated with new primer. When wet cleaning the mold it is not necessary to submerge the entire mold in water. Fill the design area with warm water and scrub with a stiff brush. After wet cleaning the mold, it must be air dried overnight or dried in the kiln at 200°F (90°C) for approximately one hour. When it is thoroughly dry and cooled it can be recoated with primer for the next firing.

# Tools, Materials and Equipment

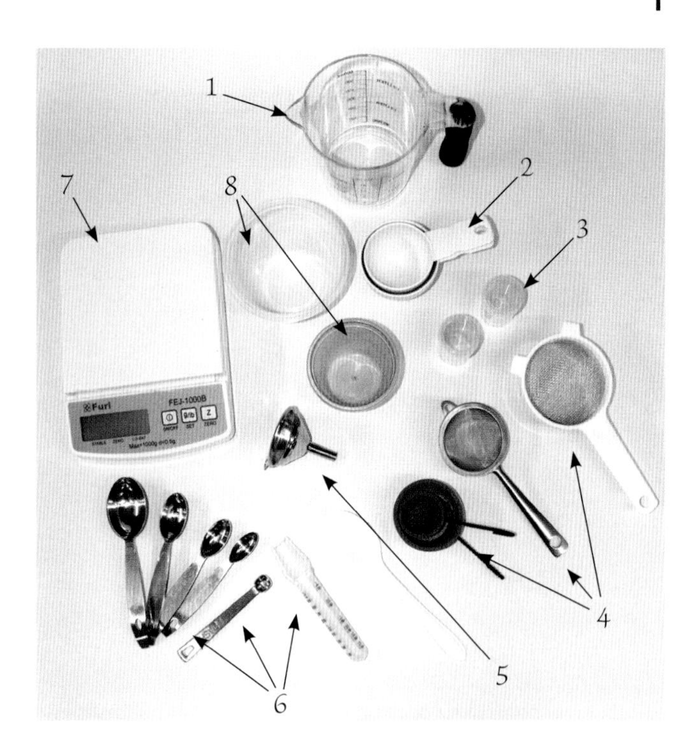


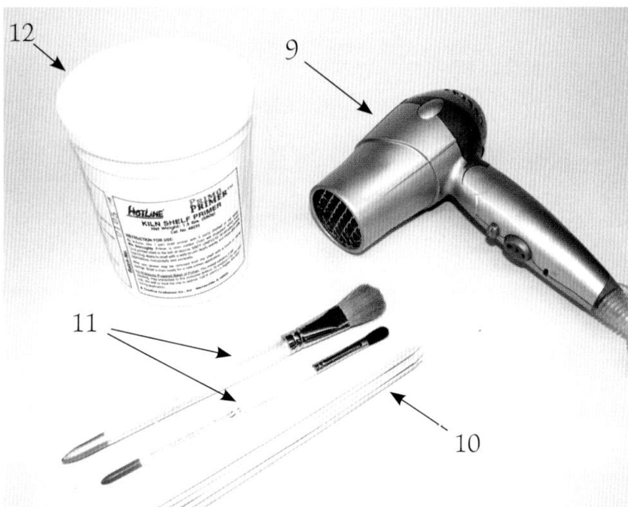


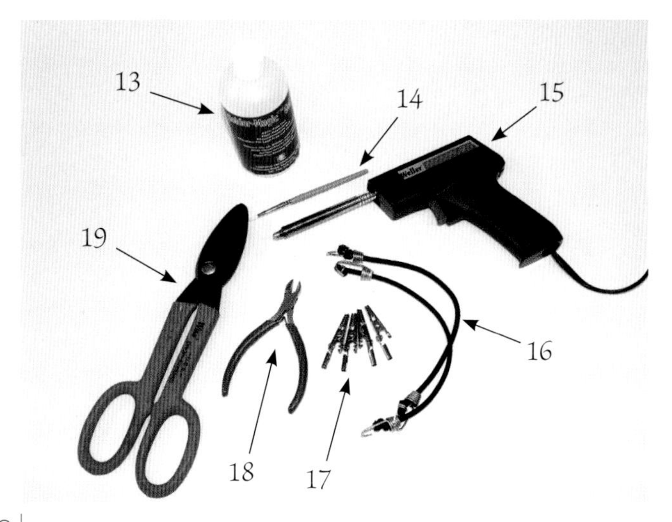


1. Measuring pitcher (with pour spout)
2. Measuring cups
3. Shaker jars (spice shakers)
4. Kitchen sieves & strainers (with assorted mesh sizes)
5. Small funnel
6. Applicator Spoons (assorted types and sizes)
7. Weigh scale (with gram measurements)
8. Small plastic bowls
9. Hairdryer
10. Wood 'shish-kebab' skewers
11. Round brushes (assorted sizes)
12. Primo Primer™
13. Soldering flux (water soluble)
14. Flux applicator brush
15. Soldering iron (wand or gun type)
16. Small bungee cords
17. Alligator clips (normally for electronics use)
18. Fine wire cutters
19. Tin shears

These small scales are available at almost any kitchen store and they are not very expensive. These scales are very easy to use but there is one really important step that you must remember. Place an empty container (like the plastic bowl in the photo above) on the scale then "ZERO' the scale by pressing the zero (or tare) button. Now when you fill it with frit the amount shown will be the frit only (and will not include the weight of the container).

# Know Your Kiln - The Key To Successful Fusing!

The title of this book is 'Glass Kiln Casting' so it should come as no surprise that a kiln is not only necessary when it come to glass casting but is without a doubt the most important tool in your fusing studio. There are dozens of styles and types of kilns available for glass fusing ranging from small tabletop models all the way up to very large production kilns. As you might expect the small 8" (20 cm) and medium kilns - up to 22" (56 cm) interior size, are the most popular for fusing artists.

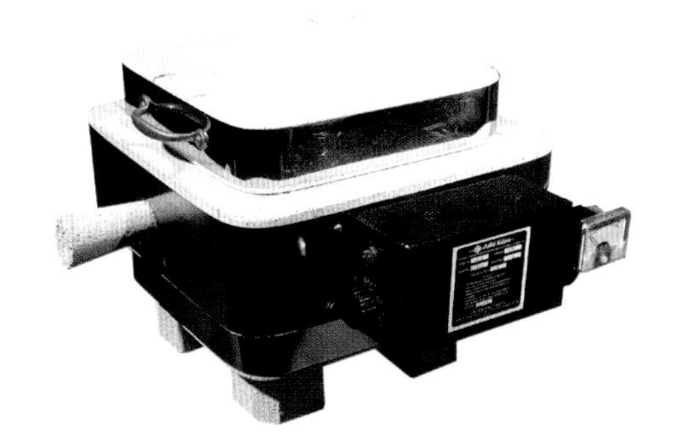

The smaller tabletop kilns have an interior size from 6" to 8" (15 to 20 cm) and are wonderful for projects like jewelry, tiles, small plates & bowls, plus other element accessories. They are also perfect for bracelet forming (we use one in chapter 12 for this) and other hot glass manipulating tasks. Small kilns are not usually equipped with automatic digital controllers instead they are controlled manually, using an infinite switch, a minute timer and the watchful eye of the operator.

## *Medium is Just Right*

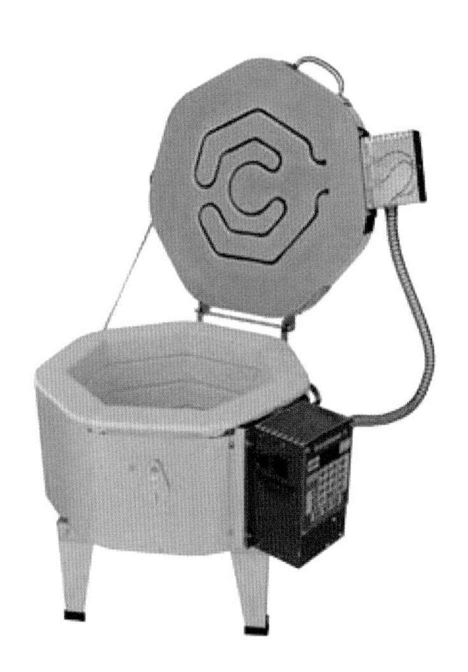

Most of the projects in this book are larger than 8" and require a medium sized kiln with an interior size of at least 15" (38 cm). In addition, the firing schedules for these projects are multi-segmented with an active cycle that could be as short as 2 hours to as much as 30 hours to complete the entire sequence. The only way to successfully perform one of these firing schedules is to use a digital kiln controller.

I am happy to report that most glass kilns in the medium to larger size category have a digital kiln controller as standard equipment. These controllers are typically preprogrammed with a few basic firing schedules. These schedules are fine for simple two layer fusing and slumping projects but are not comprehensive enough for the casting projects in this book. I have provided specific schedules for every project in this book and these must be entered into your controller.

## *Enter Step-by-Step*

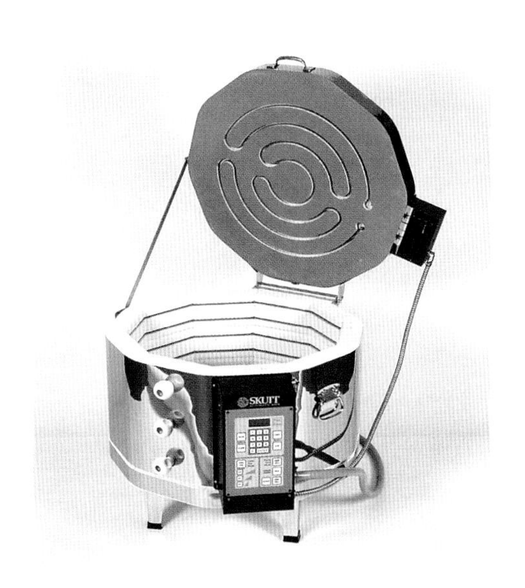


Now before your eyes glaze over let me say that the process for entering a schedule into a controller is relatively easy. In the next few pages I will walk you through the entire process, step-by-step with photographs. In the interest of full disclosure I must tell you that not all controllers will program or look exactly the same as the one I've used in my demonstration (I have a 'Rampmaster' controller). The steps will be very similar but I strongly urge you to locate the instruction manual that came with your kiln then read it to find out the specific process for entering a firing schedule into your controller.

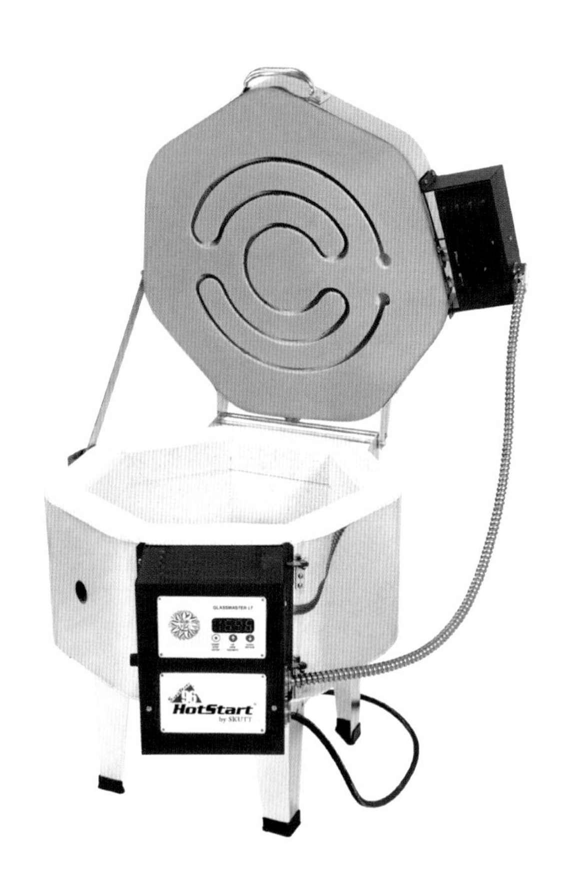


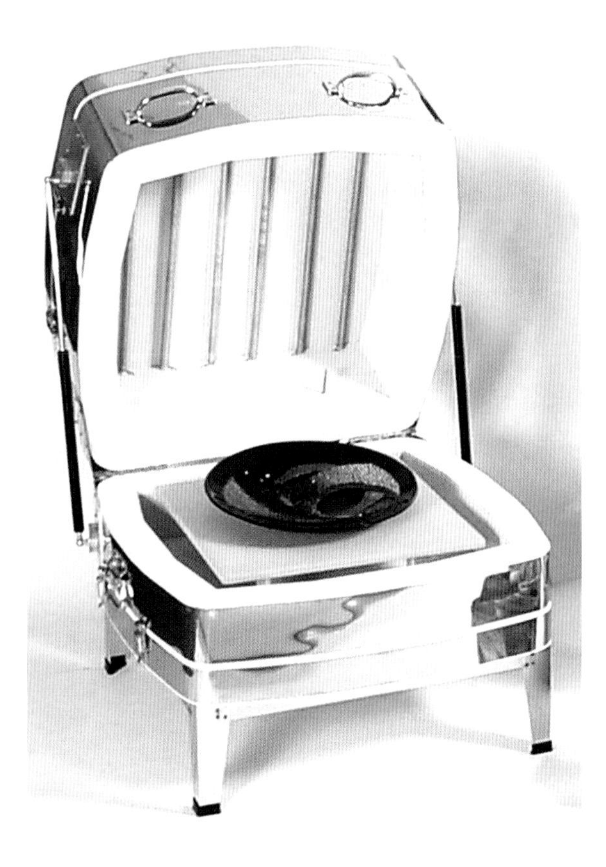

## There's Temperature - Then There's Reality

In my studio I have nine kilns made by three different manufacturers and I have worked with hundreds of different kilns in classrooms and other studios all over the world. I can honestly say that every kiln I have encountered had a slightly different optimum temperature for any given action step (slump, tack-fuse, full-fuse, etc). The temperatures were within a close range but rarely the same. So I know kilns vary in temperature but I also know that it is critical to hit the temperature for these action steps accurately. Too hot and the project could be ruined, not hot enough and it won't be what you expected. It can usually be salvaged with another firing but the first firing was a waste of time and electric power. Neither of these two options is acceptable.

## You're Within Range

You will notice that some of the firing schedules in this book list a temperature range for a key action step. This range is usually shown in the segment where the project reaches the highest temperature of the firing schedule (called the 'Target Temperature'). For example, the temperature range specified for 'Flower Casting' (see 'Segment 2' in the chart on the next page) is 1420°F - 1440°F (670°C - 782°C). Your kiln's temperature for a full-fuse casting should be somewhere within that range. In certain projects (such as chapters 5, 6 and 7) a five to ten degree variation in the 'Target Temperature' will make a big difference in the results. The projects in these chapters depend on a precise temperature that will tack fuse the cast floral components to a base glass without compromising the detailed texture of the flowers and leaves.

## You Have to Get to Know Your Kiln!

The only solution is you must know for certain the optimum temperatures for fusing, tacking, slumping, casting, etc. in your own kiln. And the only way to discover that is through test firing, critical observation and occasionally the hard way - when a firing doesn't work out! Record the temperature on your pyrometer when you observe the perfect moment for one of the action steps. Fortunately it only takes a few sample firings to determine these critical temperature points for your kiln. But it is really, really important - so I encourage you to take the time to do a temperature study on your kiln. It will pay off in the end!

# Digital Kiln Controller: Programming Basics

## *A Need To Know Basis*

I am going to show you step-by-step how I program one of my kilns (on pages 14 & 15). First we need to know the firing schedule segment details. Fortunately (for you every project in this book has its own 'Firing Schedule Chart' that lists every segment for that firing. What is important for you to know is that each segment has 3 distinct pieces of information.

| Firing Schedule for Flower Casting | | | | |
|---|---|---|---|---|
| Controller Segment | Ramp Rate (Per Hour) | Target Temperature | Heat Soak Hold Time | Interaction |
| Segment 1 | 300°F / 165°C | 1250°F / 675°C | 15 min | None |
| Segment 2 | AFAP - Up | 1420°F - 1440°F 670°C - 782°C | 20 min | Observe to Confirm Final |
| Segment 3 | AFAP - Down | 960°F / 515°C | 90 min | Don't Vent |
| Segment 4 | 60°F / 33°C ramp down | 700°F / 370°C | 1 min | Kiln Off |
| Kiln off cool down - Do not vent - Cool to room temperature before opening | | | | |

- Ramp Rate - how fast the kiln should go from it's current temperature to the target temperature - usually listed in degrees per hour, (sometimes in degrees per minute)
- Target Temperature - the temperature the kiln must reach for this particular segment
- Hold Time - how long the kiln should hold (soak) at the Target Temperature during this segment.

## *Get Your Pointer Finger Ready*

1. The first entry that the controller will require is a program number. This is a number that you assign to the firing schedule that will enable you to store it and recall it when you want to repeat the firing.
2. The next entry the controller needs is the number of segments in the firing schedule.
3. Next you'll enter the segment details; the Ramp Rate, Target Temperature and Hold Time for each segment of the firing schedule.
4. After the entries for each segment is programmed into the controller the final task is to set a safety alarm to alert you if for some reason the kiln goes above the highest 'action point' temperature. I usually set an alarm for 20°F (10°C) above the action point so if something goes wrong I will hear the alarm in time to save the firing (hopefully).

   I will use the firing schedule from Chapter 4 as the programming example. There are four segments in this firing schedule designed for casting fine frit.

- Segment 1; is a slow ramp up to 1250°F (675°C) and will be held at this temperature for 15 minutes. This segment allows the glass to heat evenly, the frit to settle and the air to escape.
- Segment 2; will ramp up to casting temperature AFAP - As Fast As Possible - we'll set the kiln to its' highest speed. Notice the temperature range listed in the chart (above) for this segment. Use the temperature that you have determined to be optimum for your kiln to cast fine frit - it should be somewhere in this range. If you don't know the optimum for your kiln then use this firing to find out - set the Target Temperature at the bottom of the range, then be in the studio to observe the casting when it gets to this temperature. Add a few degrees if necessary (most controllers have a button for that) then when the casting is perfect, record that temperature number. The kiln I am programming casts fine frit at 1420°F (770°C) so that is the temperature I will input. The hold time is 20 minutes at the casting temperature.
- Segment 3; is AFAP (As Fast As Possible) down to the annealing temperature and will be held at this temperature for 90 minutes.
- Segment 4; is a slow cool down to 700°F (370°C) with a 1 minute hold time. There is absolutely no venting during cool down.
- That's all there is to it. Now let's punch those 'Firing Schedule' numbers into the controller.

# Digital Controller: Step-by-Step Programming

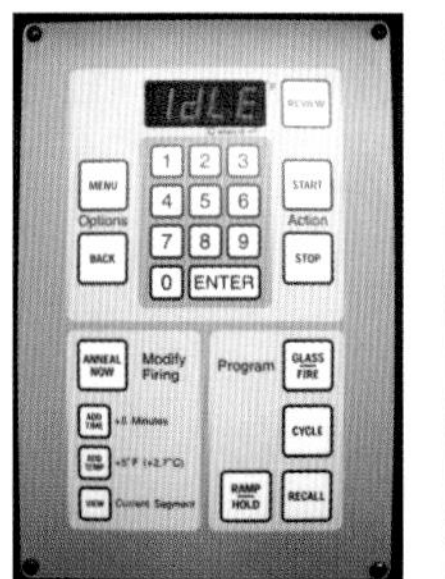

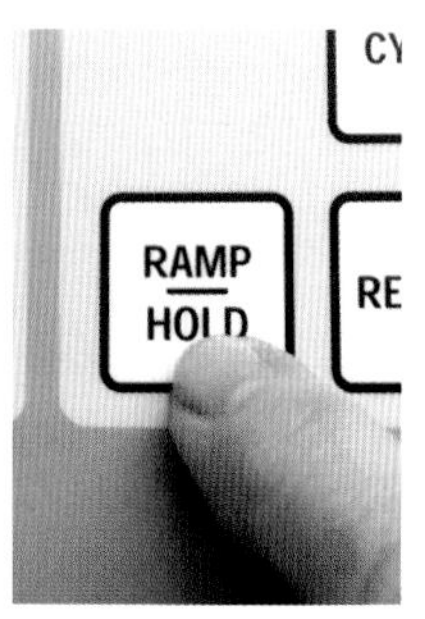

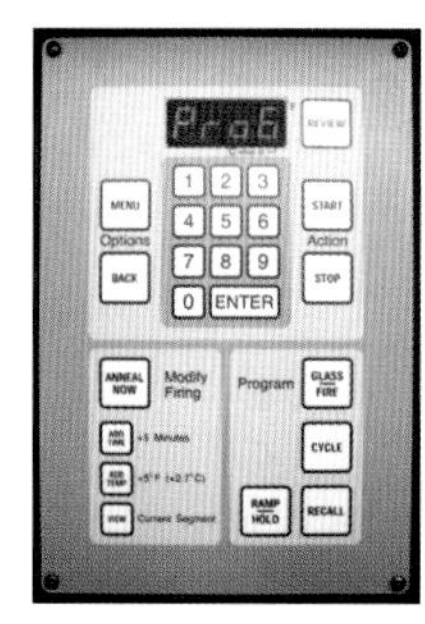


When the controller is turned on it will flash between **'IdLE'** (idle) and the current temperature inside the kiln. Press the Ramp/Hold button and **'ProG'** (Program) will appear on the screen. The controller wants a program number for this firing schedule to use to recall this program for a future firing.

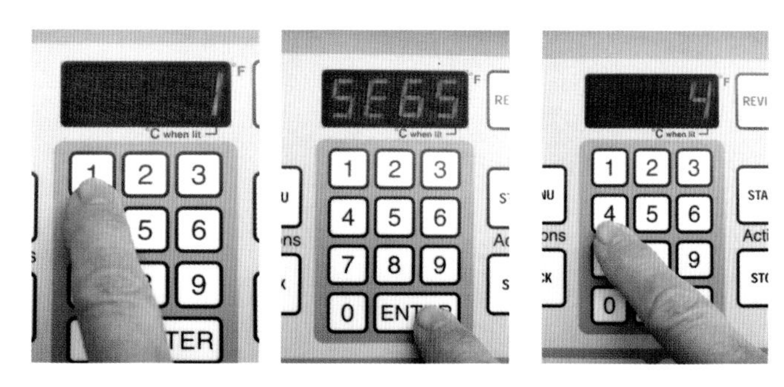


I will assign the number **1** to this firing schedule so I press the 1 button and hit Enter. **'SEGS'** (segments) will appear on the screen. The controller wants to know how many segments I want, so I check my schedule (see page 13, top right) and find it has 4, so I press the **4** button and then hit Enter.

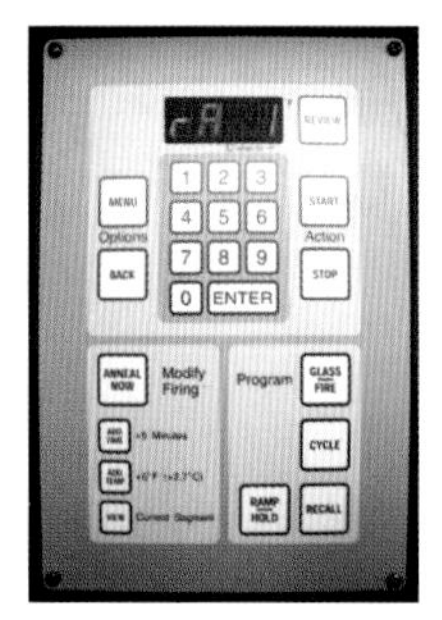

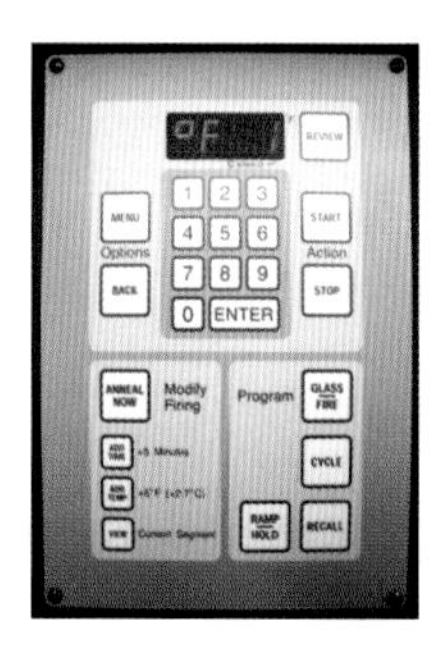


**'rA 1'** (Ramp/Rate 1) will appear on the screen. The controller wants the ramp rate for segment 1, so again I consult the firing schedule chart, then press 300 and Enter; **'°F 1'** appears on the screen.

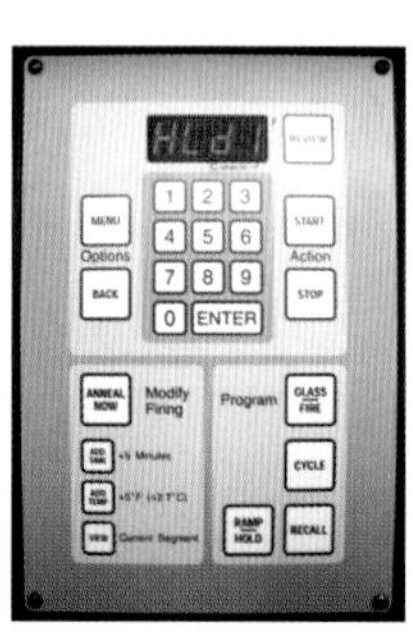

The controller is asking for the target temperature degree in Fahrenheit (°F) for segment 1 (**°F 1**), so I press 1250 and hit Enter; **'HLd1'** will appear on the screen. Now the controller wants the Hold (Soak) time for segment 1, so I press 15 and hit Enter again.

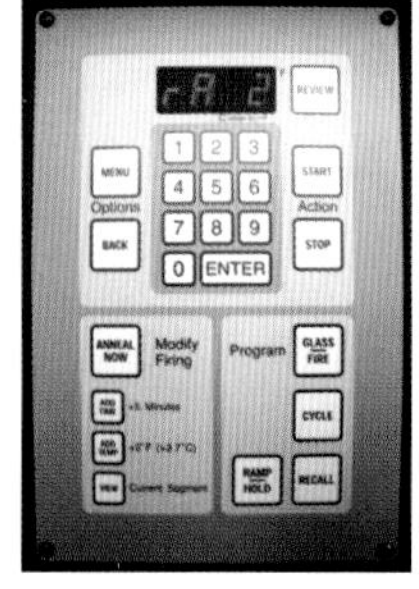

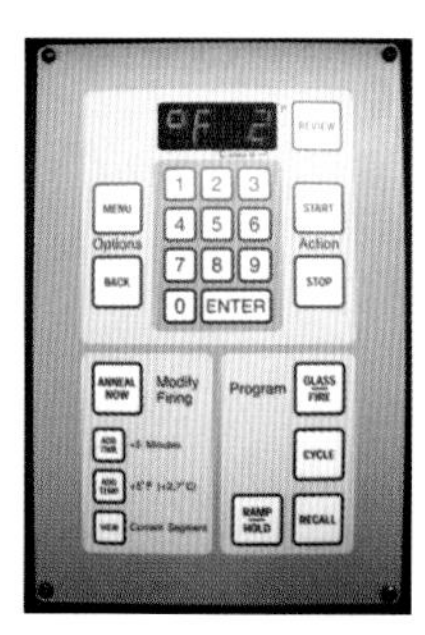


**'rA 2'** appears on the screen. Now the controller wants the ramp rate (rA) speed for segment 2, so I press 9999 and hit Enter. Why 9999? This controller uses that number for the high setting, other controllers use the code 'Full' or 'Skip' for the signal to go AFAP (check your controller's manual for the code it uses). **'°F 2'** will appear on the screen.

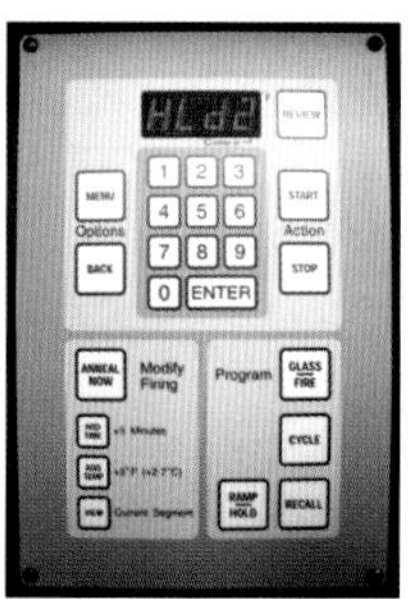

**'°F 2'** is the target temperature degree in Fahrenheit (°F) for segment 2, so I press 1420 and hit Enter; **'HLd2'** appears on the screen. That's the Hold/Soak time for segment 2, so press 20 and hit enter again. (Are you starting to see a pattern here yet?)

# Digital Controller: Step-by-Step Programming

**'rA3'** is now on the screen my schedule chart calls for AFAP down, so I press 9999 (remember, that's controller language for AFAP) and hit Enter; **'°F 3'** appears on the screen. The firing schedule tells me to set a target temperature of 960°F, so...

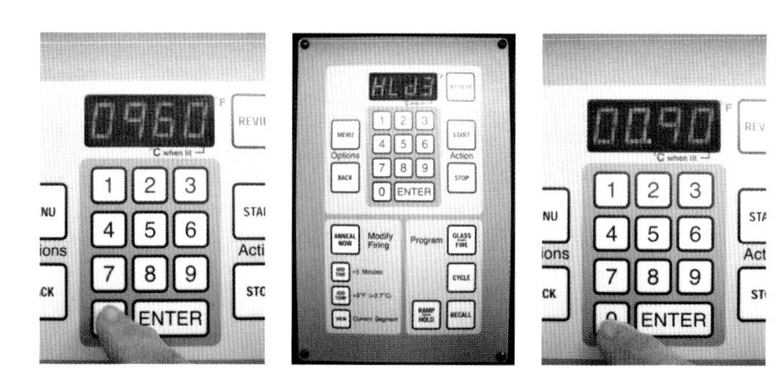


Press 960 then hit enter again. **'HLd3'** is now on the screen (hold for segment 3) so I press 90 to give me a 90 minute Hold/Soak time, then again hit Enter.

**'rA 4'** is now on the screen; that tells me the controller is looking for the ramp rate for segment 4, so I press 60 and hit Enter. **'°F 4'** appears on the screen so I check my firing chart...

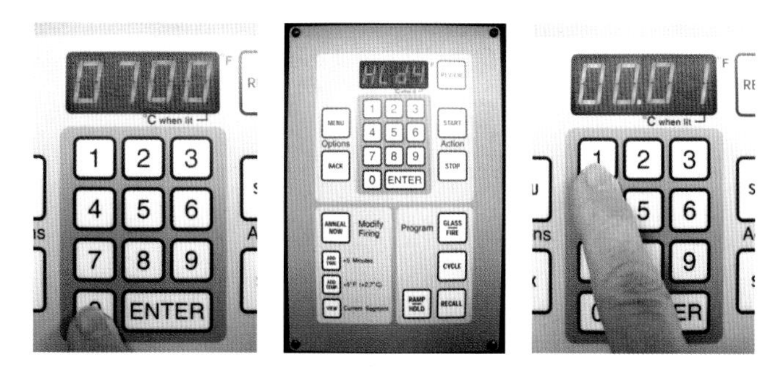


Then press 700 and hit Enter. **'HLd4'** appears on the screen now, so press 1 (for a 1 minute hold) and hit Enter (we're almost done).

**'ALAr'** will appear on the screen, as you know by now the controller is not very good at spelling - but I know it's asking for the 'Alarm' temperature. I want the controller to send an audible signal to me if it ever gets to 20°F higher than the maximum temperature on the schedule. So press 1440 and hit enter. Now **'StOP'** will appear on the screen and we've done it!

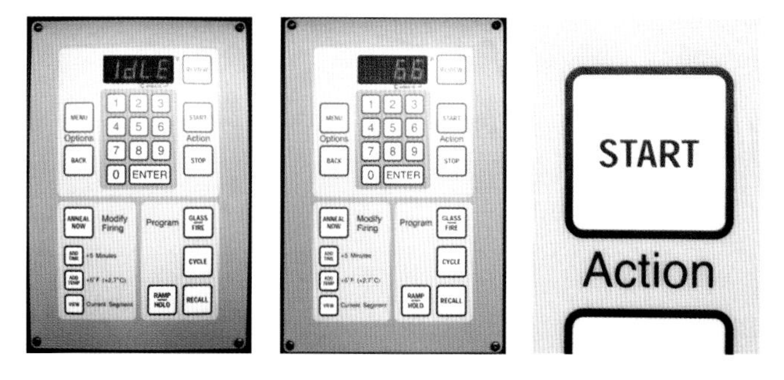


We survived the programming! The screen will now go back to flashing between to **'IdLE'** and current kiln temperature (mine was at 66°F). One final step, press the 'Review' button to check the programming to make sure you entered all the information correctly. The kiln is now read to go - Hit the START button when you have the kiln loaded and the lid shut.

# Chapter 2 - Working With Frit

## *Making Color Samples*

As I mentioned in my opening remarks on page 4, my time with Kimiake and Shinichi Higuchi at The Studio of The Corning Museum of Glass was well spent. I gained a new respect for glass frit, was introduced to a new way to think about glass designing and I had a lot of fun doing it. One of the most important points that I took away from that course was the need to make color samples to use as a reference for future work.

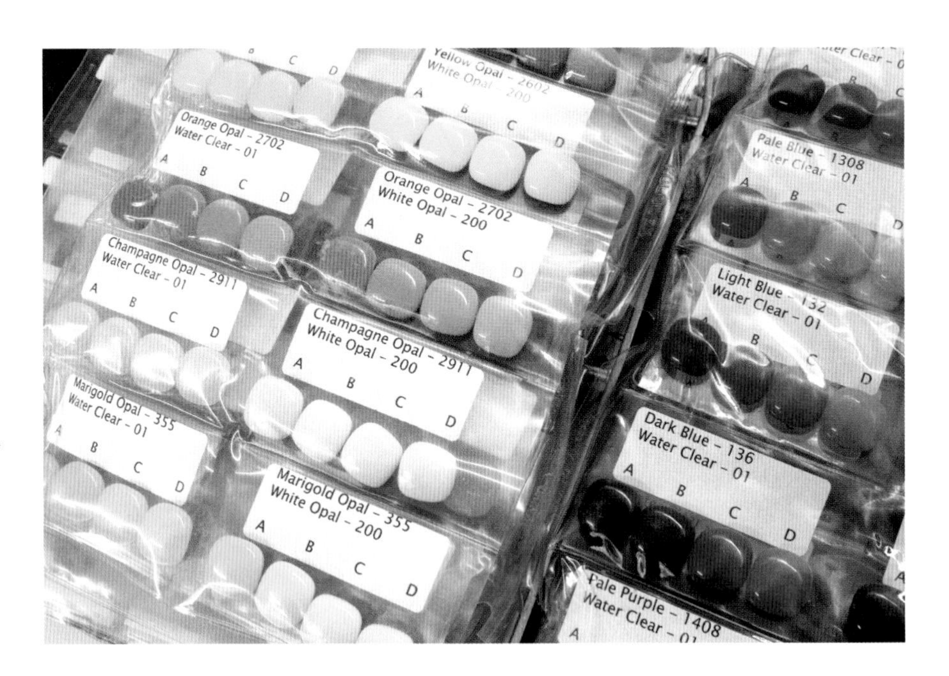


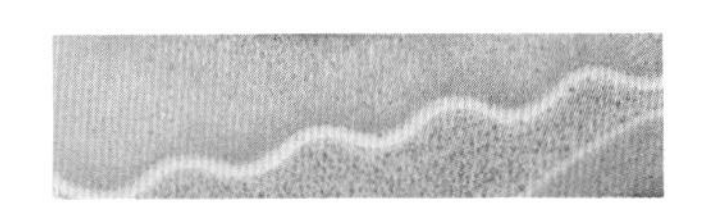

### *Tools & Equipment:*

- ***Kiln:*** Medium capacity fusing kiln with digital controller, kiln posts (assorted heights)
- ***Frit Measuring & Setting:*** Weigh scale, small plastic bowls, small funnel, applicator spoons
- ***Mold Preparation:*** Primo Primer™, applicator brush (soft, round), hairdryer
- ***Safety:*** Dust mask, safety glasses, kiln gloves

### *Materials:*

- ***Glass Supplies:*** All glass for this project must have the same COE
- Powdered Frit; clear, amber, blue, green, & orange

### *Forming Mold:*

- 'Colour de Verre' color blender mold

## *A Color Study in Frit*

When I returned to my studio after my workshop with Kimiake and Shinichi Higuchi I immediately started making color samples of all the frit that I work with. I now have several large binders with hundreds of glass samples to use as reference for all my projects. (see pages 18 & 19 for details on making color samples). This color study does require a lot of patience and time but in the end it is invaluable. Since most of my Pâte de Verre work is created with powder and fine frit, I have several sets of sample books. The first set of sample books is made with powder frit, the second set of sample books is made with fine frit, the third set of sample books is made with a combination of powder frit and fine frit and the fourth set of sample books are my own custom color blends using powder frit and fine frit. But before we get into making color samples there are a few things you need to know about frit.

First and formost is that all frit used for each project must have the same **COE** (**C**oefficient **O**f **E**xpansion). We recommend that you use only 90 COE or 96 COE in our Colour de Verre molds. The molds are not designed for Pyrex glass, float glass or crushed bottles. We don't recommend firing Colour de Verre molds above 1475°F (800°C). Firing temperatures higher than this can cause the primer to fuse and stick to both the glass and the mold and will be more difficult to remove.

Frit is available in five sizes: powder, fine, medium, coarse and mosaic. Each of these sizes will have a different look in color and opacity after being fired. The heart paperweight shown in the following photos are examples of castings made in the same mold, using the same color - the only difference is that we used five different frit sizes.

## *Frit Size Matters*

I selected the Colour de Verre heart mold for this example exercise because it creates a relatively thick casting with a smooth surface that effectively shows the outcome of the various frit sizes. I selected a transparent color called Sapphire and I used my gram scale to measure exactly 200 grams of frit for each heart.

The first heart (photo in top row) was made using powdered frit. This casting has a distinct opaque appearance even though the color used was transparent. This obscure appearance is due to air pockets that form around each individual granule of frit resulting in a large number of tiny bubbles that are trapped within the piece. As the frit size increases the quantity of bubbles decreases, enabling the light to pass through the casting more directly. The outcome is an object with more apparent clarity.

Each heart paperweight shown at right was made using 200 grams of Sapphire colored frit. They all used 100% color with no clear mixed in. The only variation from casting to casting was the frit particle size, as specified below:

Row 1 • Powder frit

Row 2 • Fine frit

Row 3 • Medium frit

Row 4 • Coarse frit

Row 5 • Mosaic frit

## *Frit Blending for Color Variation*

I have taught this technique to thousands of artists and in almost every case people are surprised by how much darker the resulting color is than they were expecting. The color of the frit in the jar usually appears lighter than it will be after it has been fired and cast. Depending on the frit color and grit size this difference can be substantial. For this reason it is essential for you to produce a series of color samples to create both a color reference and a mixture formula that will enable you to repeat a particular color shade.

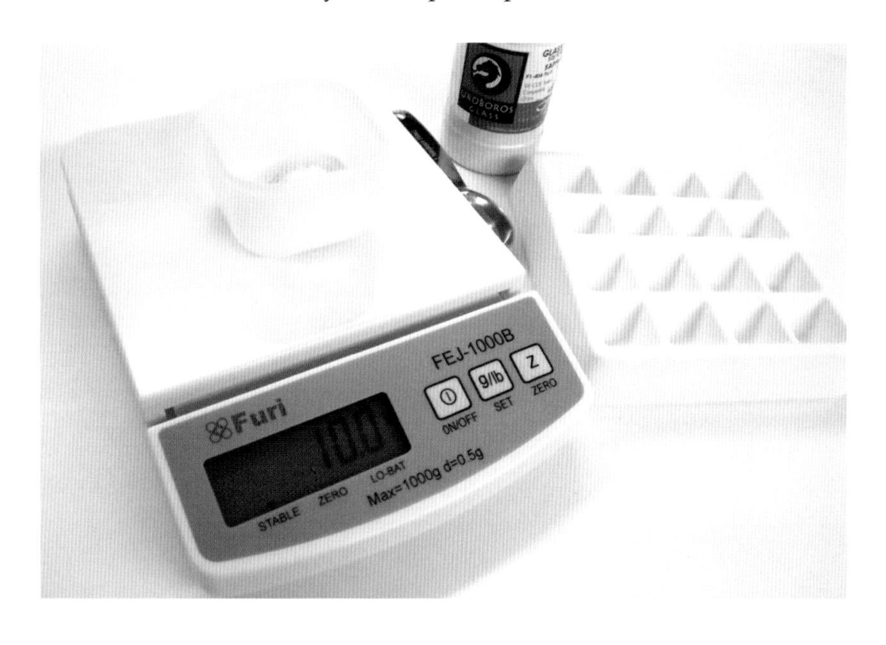

## *How It's Done*

1. Before you start mixing the frit for this exercise you will need to coat the 'Colour de Verre' color blender mold with four coats of primer and dry it with a hairdryer (see 'Mold Preparation' on page 8).
2. The color blender has 16 sections. I selected four powdered frit colors (amber, blue, green & orange) to fill this mold. The sections in the first column (from top to bottom) will be A mixes, the sections in the second column will be B mixes, the sections in the third column will be C mixes and the sections in the fourth column will be D mixes.
3. We will mix four different percentages of each color. The first mix (A) will be a 50% mix (50% color & 50% clear). The second mix (B) will be a 20% mix (20% color & 80% clear). The third mix (C) will be a 10% mix (10% color & 90% clear). The fourth mix (D) will be a 5% mix (5% color and 95% clear).
4. It takes approximately 7 grams of frit to fill each section but it is easier to 'do the math' when mixing 10 grams of each color blend. So, for 10 grams of frit total, the mixtures will be as follows:

   A Mix (Column 1) - 5 grams of color and 5 grams of clear.

   B Mix (Column 2)- 2 grams of color and 8 grams of clear.

   C Mix (Column 3)- 1 gram of color and 9 grams of clear.

   D Mix (Column 4)- 0.5 grams of color and 9.5 grams of clear.
5. Fill each section with 7 grams of frit. I like to use a small funnel for this step. It helps to control the frit, keeping it neatly in each section.

6. Lay three kiln posts on their side on the kiln shelf to elevate the mold during the firing. Carefully position the filled mold on the kiln posts and check the mold for level and stability. I keep a small level near my kiln to check the mold before each firing.
7. Close the kiln and program your kiln controller according to the firing schedule on this page. For more information on controller programming procedures see page 12 & 13.
8. When the firing is complete and the kiln has shut off, you must allow the kiln to cool completely to room temperature without venting. Any exposure to cool air, even a quick peek, could produce thermal shock. It's not worth the risk, just leave the kiln alone and come back when it has safely cooled.
9. At right is a photo of our color samples still in the blender mold after firing. The color variation is a result of the color to clear mixture. The percent number on the photo is the quantity of color used in each column.
10. The final step is to organize your finished samples in a binder. I like to use the clear plastic holder sheets designed to organize business cards. Be sure to mark the color name, number and frit size for both frits that you use in every mixture. I have come to rely on this color sample binder whenever I'm trying to decide on a color combination for a frit casting.

| Firing Schedule for Colour Blender | | | | |
|---|---|---|---|---|
| Controller Segment | Ramp Rate (Per Hour) | Target Temperature | Heat Soak Hold Time | Interaction |
| Segment 1 | 300°F / 165°C | 1420°F - 1440°F<br>770°C - 782°C | 10 to 15 minutes | Kiln Off |
| Kiln off cool down - Do not vent - Cool to room temperature before opening | | | | |

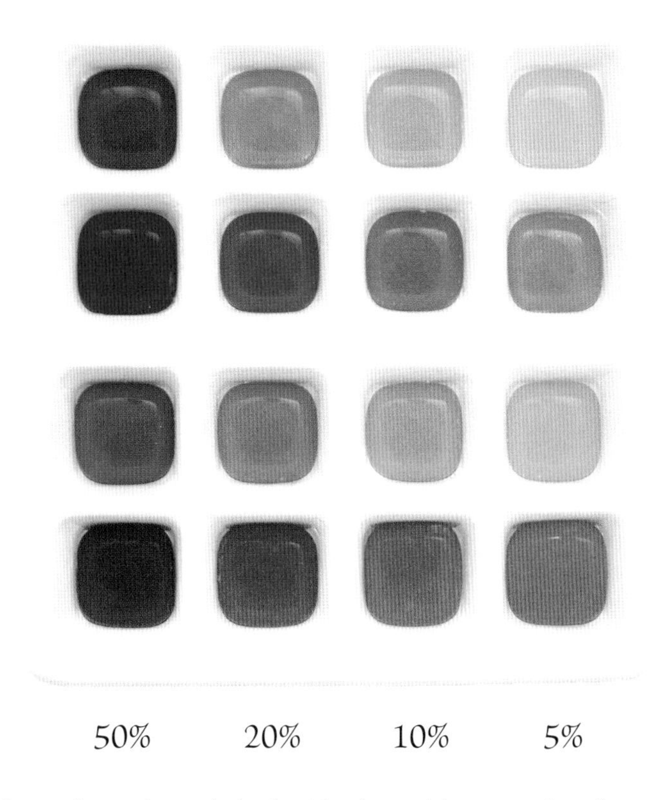


*Finished samples in the cooled color blender mold. Notice the color variation we achieved by mixing clear frit with the colored frit. The percentage number shown on the photo is the amount of color frit that was used in the mix.*

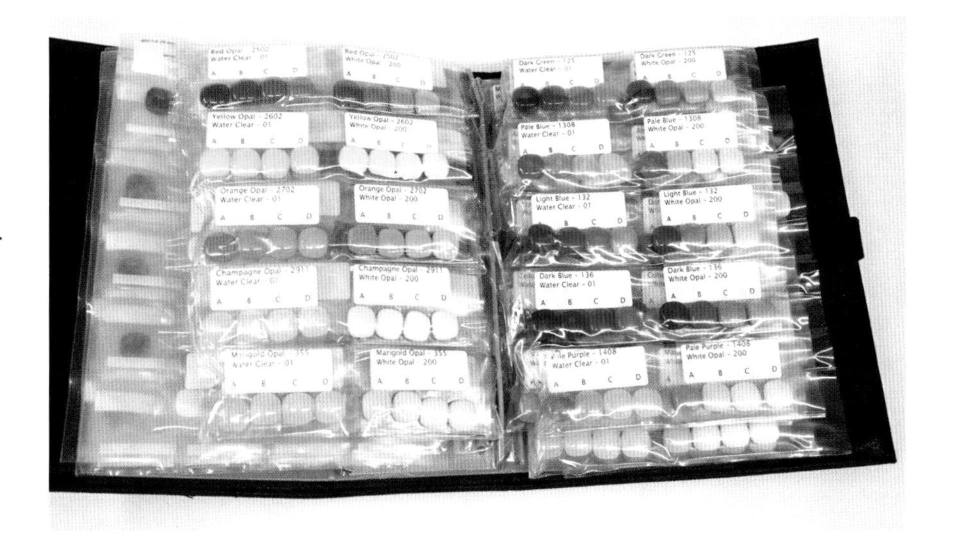

# Chapter 3 - Butterflies and Dragonflies

The Butterfly and Dragonfly molds are the most popular Colour de Verre molds. These projects are a great place to start when learning to work with frit. Not only are they attractive and colorful they look great hanging in a window or just sitting on your desk. They can be slumped and work well when combined in component projects - see Showcase Galleries on pages 24 & 25. The first project that we will make in this chapter is a large butterfly. The second project is two small dragonflies that will be cast and slumped using the same mold.

### *Tools & Equipment:*

- ***Kiln:*** Medium capacity fusing kiln with digital controller, kiln posts (assorted heights)
- ***Frit Measuring & Setting:*** Weigh scale, small plastic bowls, measuring pitcher (with pour spout), measuring cup, measuring spoons, small funnel, small kitchen sieve (mesh for powder), applicator spoons
- ***Mold Preparation:*** Primo Primer™, applicator brush (soft, round), hairdryer
- ***Safety:*** Dust mask, safety glasses, kiln gloves
- ***Glass Cutting and Shaping:*** Diamond polishing pad

### *Materials:*

- ***Glass Supplies:*** All glass for this project must have the same COE
- Powdered Frit; light green, medium green, dark green
- Fine Frit; pink, aqua, neon-orchid
- Clear dichroic sheet - Thin 1/16″ (1.5 mm) - small piece

### *Forming Molds:*

- 'Colour de Verre' large butterfly mold
- 'Colour de Verre' small dragonfly mold

## *The Butterfly*

**1**. Prepare the butterfly mold with primer, mixed and applied as discussed in chapter 1 on pages 8 & 9. Be sure to dry the primer between coats with a handheld hairdryer and then again after the last coat.

**2**. The first layer of glass frit placed into the mold is the topside of the butterfly. This is because the texture and design is in the bottom of the mold and the glass frit will form into this design texture when it has reached casting temperature. When the casting is removed it will be turned right side up to reveal the mirror image of the design in the bottom of the mold. This is true for all Colour de Verre projects, the first colors you put into the mold will be on the top or 'front-side' of your finished casting. To give this project a little spark I cut four small oval shapes using thin clear dichroic glass and place them in the wing sections with the coated dichroic side down against the mold. Then I filled the body cavity of the butterfly with some dark green powder frit.

**3**. Now use a small kitchen sieve (fine mesh for powder size frit) to sift a small amount of the dark green powder frit out towards the center of the wings. Then sift a larger amount of light green powder frit over the center portion of the butterfly.

4. Finish by filling the rest of the butterfly mold with 90 grams of pink fine frit. Use a small brush around the perimeter of each butterfly to move some of the frit away from the outside edge of the mold to create a slight channel all the way around. Be sure to leave the frit at least 1/8" (3 mm) deep. This channel will encourage a smoother edge when the piece is fired.
5. Elevate the butterfly mold by placing it on 3 kiln posts (laying on their side) in the kiln.
6. Close the kiln and program your kiln controller according to the firing schedule on this page. For more information on controller programming procedures see page 12 & 13.
8. When the firing is complete and the kiln has shut off, you must allow the kiln to cool completely to room temperature without venting. Any exposure to cool air could produce thermal shock. Simply leave the kiln alone and come back when it has safely cooled.
9. Remove the butterfly by turning the mold upside down, it should fall out easily, if it doesn't don't panic. Lay a soft towel (or some newspaper) on your bench then turn the mold over and tap it against the cushioned surface. If that doesn't do it, see ProTip on page 23 for more ideas.

*Photo far right: A view of the finished butterfly. Notice the dichroic strips in the wings and the subtle gradation of green out from the body. Frit casting gives you an opportunity to create some realistic effects.*

### ProTip: Frit Placement

The best effects are achieved when you can precisely control the placement of the frit. Try using a variety of small spoons, a small funnel, an applicator 'squirt' bottle (with a small opening), salt shakers, various sized kitchen sieves or any number of other items that you may find useful. You could use one or more of these in a single project, depending on the effect you're looking for.

**Firing Schedule for Frit Casting Small Projects**

| Controller Segment | Ramp Rate (Per Hour) | Target Temperature | Heat Soak Hold Time | Interaction |
|---|---|---|---|---|
| Segment 1 | 300°F / 165°C | 1250°F / 675°C | 10 min | None |
| Segment 2 | AFAP Up | 1420°F / 770°C | 10 - 20 minutes | Observe to Confirm Final |
| Segment 3 | AFAP Down | 960°F / 515°C | 45 min | Kiln Off |
| Kiln off cool down - Do not vent - Cool to room temperature before opening | | | | |

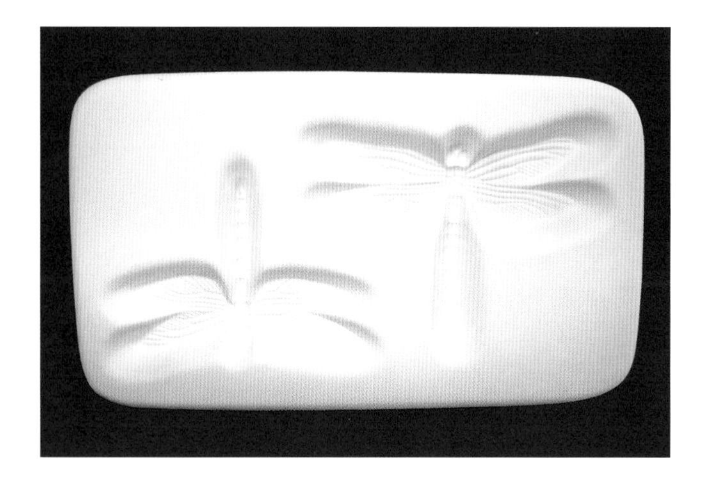

## *Two Dragonflies*

**1**. Prepare the dragonfly mold with primer, mixed and applied as discussed in chapter 1 on pages 8 & 9. Be sure to dry the primer between coats with a hairdryer and then again after the last coat.

**2**. Fill one of the dragonfly bodies with medium green powder frit then sift aqua powder frit across the wings. Fill the other dragonfly body with aqua powder frit and sift medium green powder frit across the wings.

**3**. Back fill the small dragonfly with 15 grams of neon-orchid fine frit and back fill the larger dragonfly with 25 grams of neon orchid fine frit.

**4**. Place the mold on 3 kiln posts (laying on their side) in the kiln. Close the kiln and program your kiln controller according to the firing schedule on page 21 for 'Frit Casting Small Projects.'

**Note:** If you have room in your kiln you could fire both the butterfly project and this dragonfly project in the same firing.

*The photo at left shows the back view of finished dragonflies while they are still in the mold after firing.*

*Photo above is the top view (textured side) of the finished dragonflies after removal from the casting mold.*

## *Slumping The Wings For A Realistic Effect*

1. The small dragonfly mold has a built in wing slumper on the bottom side. Coat this 'slumping' side with two coats of primer and dry with a hairdryer.
2. Place the mold in the kiln and elevate it on 3 kiln posts (laying on their side). Place the dragonflies on the mold textured side up as shown in the photo.
3. Close the kiln and set your kiln controller according to the firing schedule below right.

| Firing Schedule for Slumping Dragonflies | | | | |
|---|---|---|---|---|
| Controller Segment | Ramp Rate (Per Hour) | Target Temperature | Heat Soak Hold Time | Interaction |
| Segment 1 | 300°F / 165°C | 1200°F / 650°C | 10 min | Observe to Confirm Final |
| Segment 2 | AFAP Down | 960°F / 515°C | 30 min | Kiln Off |
| Kiln off cool down - Do not vent - Cool to room temperature before opening | | | | |

### *ProTip: When a Casting Gets Stuck in a Mold*

It doesn't happen very often but sometimes a casting gets stuck, when a few gentle taps against your hand isn't enough to persuade your piece to release. This means your casting has fused to the mold during firing and mold release (primer) malfunction is almost always the cause of this problem. Make sure you used Primo Primer™ for glass kiln casting. If you did, then either the mold wasn't fully coated with primer or it wasn't fully dried before it was fired. The other possibility is the casting temperature was too hot. A casting temperature that exceeds 1475°F (800°C) can cause the primer to stick to both the glass and the mold. This is especially true if the project was held at this temperature for a longer time.

So what can you do about a stubbornly stuck casting? First lay a soft towel (or several thicknesses of newspaper) on your bench. Then put on your safety glasses & leather gloves and cross your fingers (I know that's hard to do with gloves on). Now grasp the mold with a gloved hand, turn it upside down, take a deep breath and thump it face down on your covered bench (not too hard but with conviction). If that doesn't do it, try thumping it down again. Still no luck? Give it a one last try, but be careful that you don't bang it down so hard that you smash (or crack) the mold, sending dangerous fragments of ceramic and glass everywhere. If the casting hasn't dislodged after a few stern thumps then it may be time to face the unavoidable truth. Chalk one up to experience and resolve to do a better job of cleaning, coating and firing the next mold.

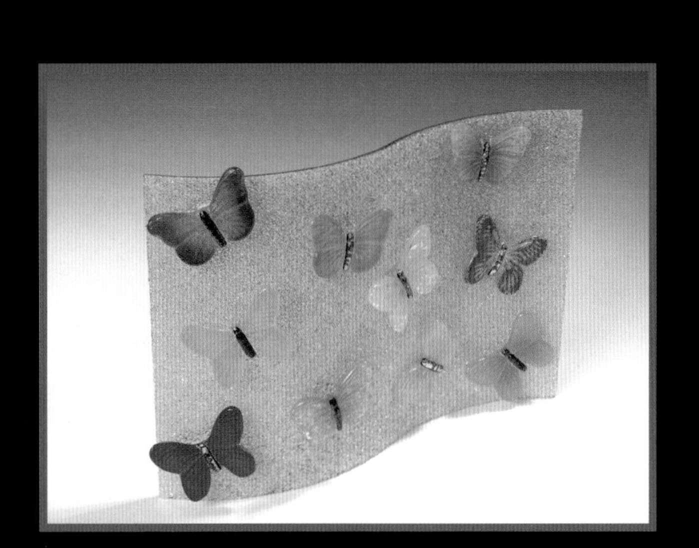

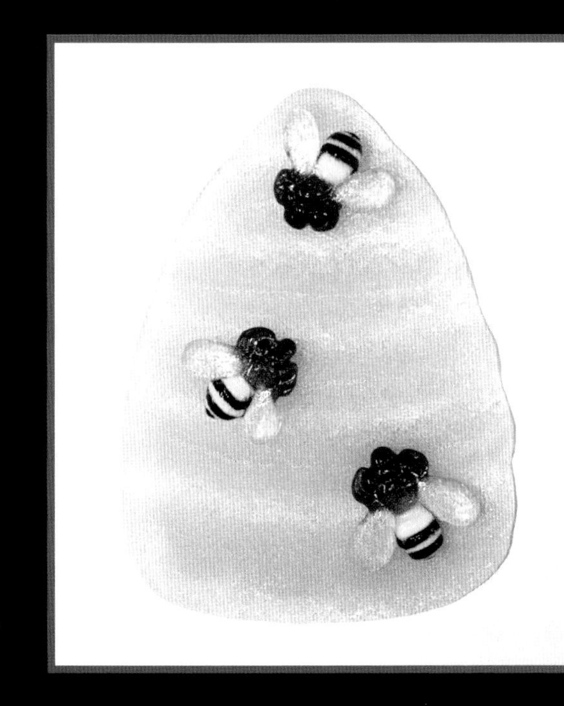

# Chapter 4 - Summer Floral Bowl

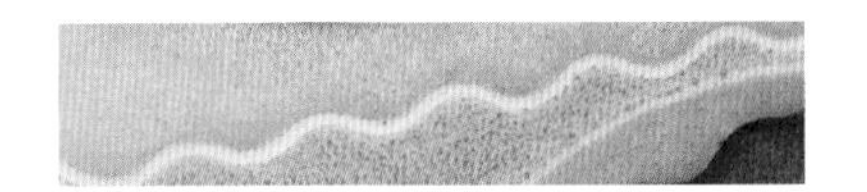

***Tools & Equipment:***

- ***Kiln:*** Medium capacity fusing kiln with digital controller, kiln posts (assorted heights)
- ***Frit Measuring & Setting:*** Weigh scale, small plastic bowls, measuring pitcher (with pour spout), measuring cup, measuring spoons, small funnel, kitchen sieves & strainers (with assorted mesh sizes), applicator spoons
- ***Mold Preparation:*** Primo Primer™, applicator brush (soft, round), hairdryer, wood 'shish-kebab' skewer
- ***Safety:*** Dust mask, safety glasses, kiln gloves
- ***Glass Cutting and Shaping:*** glass grinder with standard bit, diamond polishing pad

***Materials:***

- ***Glass Supplies:*** All glass for this project must have the same COE
- Fine Frit; clear, clear dichroic, blue, light green, dark green

***Forming Molds:***

- 'Colour de Verre' summer floral mold
- 'Colour de Verre' 12" (30 cm) bowl slumping mold or 10" (25.5 cm) plate slumping mold

## *Filling a Large Colour de Verre Mold*

Colour de Verre currently has three floral plate designs, Rose, Summer Floral and Plain Floral. The Summer Floral is a very popular design with a flower that is approximately 9" (23 cm) in diameter. For this project we will make a bowl however the Summer Flower can also be slumped into a shallow plate form that would work together with the bowl as a set. When the Plain Floral design is made into a green leaf plate it is the perfect compliment under a colorful Rose or Summer Floral bowl. This project requires a total of 500 grams of frit and can be filled many ways. We will be creating a blue flower with a dichroic center and green leaves. I am using this color suggestion so that you can see how to divide the flower (500 grams) into three sections; center (50 grams), flower (300 grams) and leaves (150 grams). The color for the flower and leaves will be further divided with decorative shading.

## *How It's Done*

**1.** Prepare the summer floral casting mold with primer following the process on page 8 & 9. Primer separates quickly and will settle and thicken on the bottom of the container so each time you dip your brush into the container be sure to give it a stir.

**2.** Dry the primer with a hair dryer between each coat. You can tell the primer is dry when it becomes lighter in color. Apply a total of four to five thin coats of primer on a new mold. A previously coated and used mold needs to be cleaned then have three thin coats of primer applied

## *ProTip: Is the Mold Dry Yet?*

Sometimes the mold will continue to feel damp even after you have painstakingly dried it with your hair dryer between each primer coat and again after the final coat. This is especially true for artists who live in an area with high humidity. As you know by now, it is very important that the mold be thoroughly dry before firing it. The best solution is to dry the mold in your kiln at 200°F (93°C) for about an hour. Drying the mold at a temperature higher than this could damage the effectiveness of the primer.

3. The only accurate way to control the color mix is to weigh the frit using a gram scale. This project requires approximately 500 grams of frit in total. 50 grams of dichroic frit for the center of the flower, 175 grams of fine blue frit for the flower petals, 125 grams of fine clear frit for the flower petals, 75 grams of fine light green frit for half of the leaf petals, and 75 grams of fine dark green frit for the remaining leaf petals. Don't forget to press the zero button (aka tare weight) on the scale after you have placed the bowl but before you add any frit!

4. The center of the flower will be dichroic. Manufactured Dichroic frit is available only in medium/coarse size (see ProTip below). If it is placed in the mold first it may make the surface of the flower rough. Therefore, to create a smooth finish I sprinkle a small amount of fine frit in the mold prior to adding the dichroic frit. For this project I used some of the fine blue frit first. Then I carefully piled 50 grams of the dichroic frit in the center of the flower.

## *ProTip: DIY Dichroic Frit*

Manufactured dichroic frit is significantly different than the 'Do-It-Yourself' frit you make in your studio by crushing dichroic sheet glass. Studio crushed frit only has dichroic coating on one surface. However, the manufactured variety is coated after the frit is crushed, so the dichroic coating will be on several surfaces of the glass particles. When fired, the effect is noticeably different. The manufactured frit has more dimension and expression, while the studio made frit has more separation and less depth. When I am using DIY studio made dichroic frit I find it helps to place some of the larger pieces on edge to encourage a more intense look.

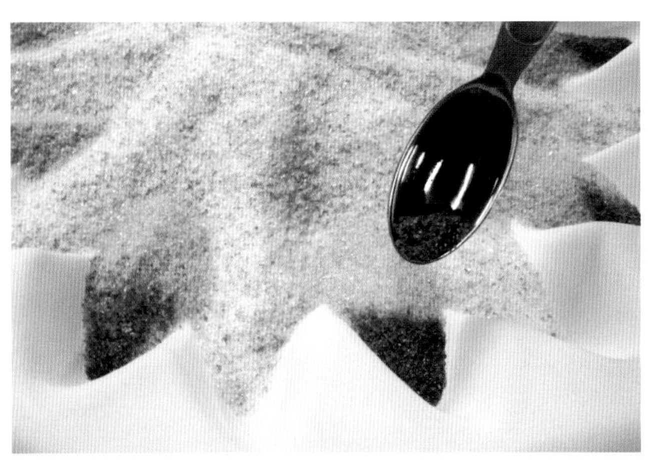

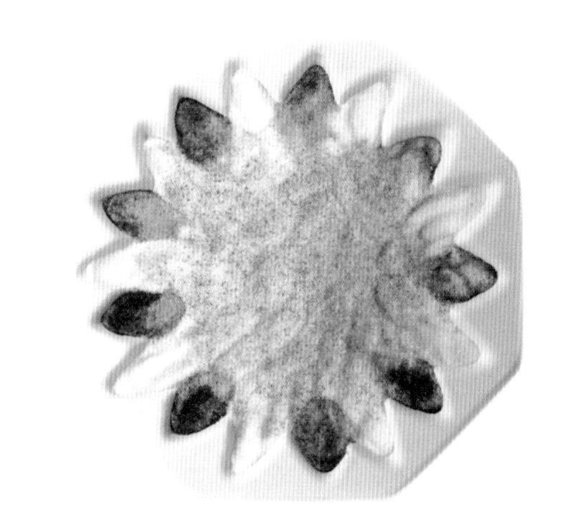

5. Now add 175 grams of fine blue frit to the flower center and flower petals. Carefully pile the frit to make it thicker in the center of the flower and taper off to a thinner layer at the tips of the flower petals. Clear frit will be added to the tips of the flower petals after the leaf petals are filled.
6. The sepal leaves are filled with dark green frit at the tips and light green frit closer to the flower center. This is done in layers. Start with the dark green frit at the tips and extend it to the center of the leaf. The light green frit is then added to the leaves starting from the blue flower petals and extending to the center of the leaf, blending over the dark green. Layer each leaf in this manner until all are filled. This blending technique will give the leaves a more natural look.
7. Finish by adding clear frit to the tips of the flower petals. Extend a thin layer of the clear frit over the blue frit towards the center of the flower. The clear frit will be thicker at the tips of the flower and taper off to blend in with the blue frit. This will give the flower petals a natural gradation.
8. Lay three kiln posts on their side on the kiln shelf to elevate the mold during the firing. If you have a shallow kiln remove the kiln shelf and place the kiln posts directly on the kiln floor and then place the mold on the posts. It is important that the mold is not too close to the heating elements in the lid as this will produce uneven heating and could cause the mold to crack.
9. Carefully position the floral mold on the kiln posts (laying on their side) and check the mold for level and stability. I keep a small level near my kiln to check the mold before each firing.

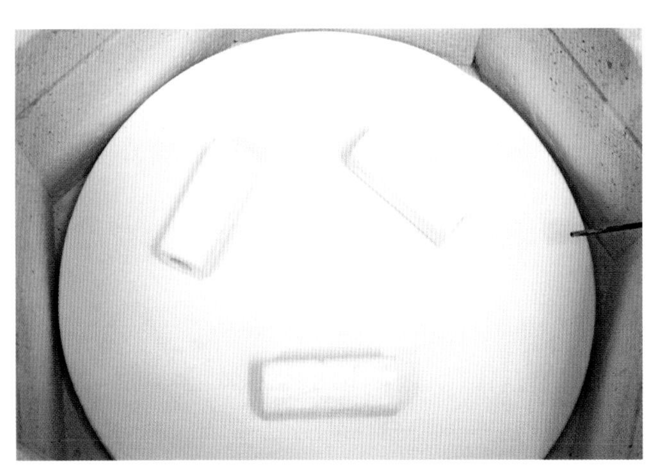

10. Close the kiln and program your kiln controller according to the firing schedule for 'Flower Casting.'

11. When the flower casting has cooled it is ready to be slumped into the bowl form. If you find any spikes or sharp points on the edge of the casting file them down with a diamond pad or grind them lightly with your glass grinder. Don't worry if the sanding or grinding produces a few rough dull spots, these minor imperfections will polish out during the slumping process.

12. Prepare the bowl slumping mold (or the plate mold) with two coats of primer and dry it well. Poke a skewer through the vent hole to be sure it's open (see ProTip on page 33 for more on mold vents). Set the mold on the kiln posts and make sure the mold is not too close to the elements.

13. Carefully center the flower casting on the slumping mold and you're ready to begin the slumping process. Close the kiln and program your controller according to the firing schedule for slumping below.

**Firing Schedule for Flower Casting**

| Controller Segment | Ramp Rate (Per Hour) | Target Temperature | Heat Soak Hold Time | Interaction |
|---|---|---|---|---|
| Segment 1 | 300°F / 165°C | 1250°F / 675°C | 15 min | None |
| Segment 2 | AFAP - Up | 1420°F - 1440°F<br>670°C - 782°C | 20 min | Observe to Confirm Final |
| Segment 3 | AFAP - Down | 960°F / 515°C | 90 min | Don't Vent |
| Segment 4 | 60°F / 33°C ramp down | 700°F / 370°C | 1 min | Kiln Off |
| Kiln off cool down - Do not vent - Cool to room temperature before opening | | | | |

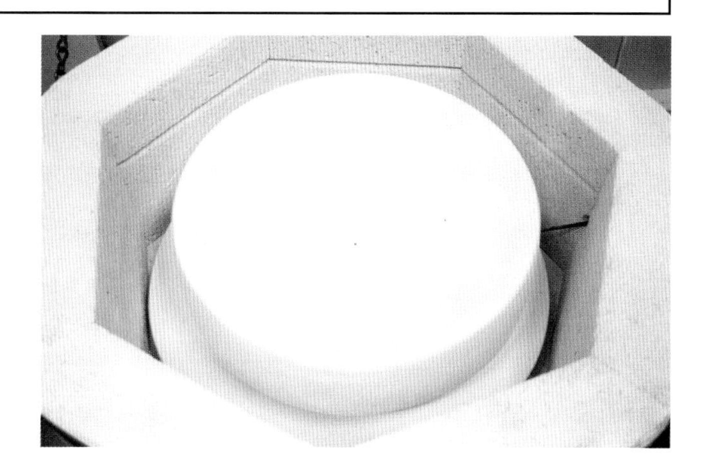

**Firing Schedule for Flower Slumping**

| Controller Segment | Ramp Rate (Per Hour) | Target Temperature | Heat Soak Hold Time | Interaction |
|---|---|---|---|---|
| Segment 1 | 200°F / 110°C | 1200°F - 1220°F<br>650°C - 660°C | 10 min | Observe to Confirm Final |
| Segment 2 | AFAP - Down | 960°F / 515°C | 90 min | Don't Vent |
| Segment 3 | 60°F / 33°C Ramp Down | 700°F / 370°C | 1 min | Kiln Off |
| Kiln off cool down - Do not vent - Cool to room temperature before opening | | | | |

*The slumped and finished Summer Floral bowl (shown above, still in the slumping mold) exhibits beautiful gradations, from the intense dichroic center to the darker blue mid-section extending out to the delicate light blue tips. The gradation in the green sepals is a result of the subtle mixing of the light green and dark green frit that we carefully placed in step 6.*

# Chapter 5 - Snowflake Plate and Goblet

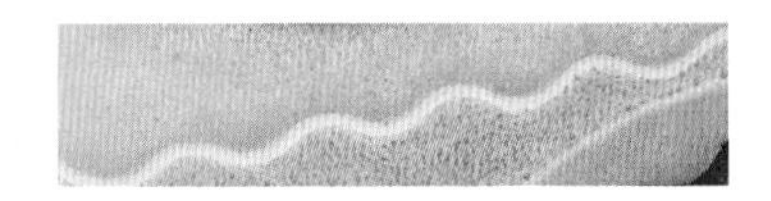

### Tools & Equipment:

- ***Kiln:*** Medium capacity fusing kiln with digital controller, kiln posts (assorted heights)
- ***Frit Measuring & Setting:*** Weigh scale, small plastic bowls, measuring pitcher (with pour spout), measuring cup, measuring spoons, small funnel, kitchen sieves & strainers (with assorted mesh sizes), applicator spoons
- ***Mold Preparation:*** Primo Primer™, applicator brush (soft, round), hairdryer, wood 'shish-kebab' skewer
- ***Safety:*** Dust mask, safety glasses, kiln gloves
- ***Glass Cutting and Shaping:*** Glasscutter, circle cutter tool, breaking pliers, fine wire cutters, glass grinder with standard bit (or glass grinder with a flat disc), grinder with 'ripple glass' edging bit, diamond polishing pad, diamond blade glass saw

### Materials:

- ***Adhesive:*** Ultraviolet Adhesive, Ultraviolet Curing Lamp
- ***Glass Supplies:*** All glass for this project must have the same COE

- Fine Frit; medium green
- Medium Frit; clear
- Clear dichroic sheet - Thin (1.5 mm)
- Clear iridized sheet - Std thick (3 mm), at least 10″ (25.4 cm) square for each plate
- Stemware goblet

### Forming Mold:

- 'Colour de Verre' snowflake mold
- Plate slump mold 10″ (25.5 cm)

## *Single Component Project*

This chapter will explain how to incorporate a single cast component into a slumped plate design. Plus I'll show you how to replace the foot of a stemware goblet to create a unique base. We will make a series of thin snowflakes with dichroic accents using one of the Colour de Verre snowflake molds. We'll tack fuse some of our snowflakes onto plates and others will be fastened to the base of commercial wineglasses using ultraviolet adhesive. Both of these creations are perfect winter holiday projects that would make any celebration festive and delightful!

## *Creating The Snowflakes*

1. Prepare the mold with primer as shown on pages 8 & 9. Remember to stir the mixture each time you dip your brush to keep it mixed well. A new mold should have 5 thin coats of primer while an already fired mold needs only 3 coats. Thoroughly dry the primer with a handheld hair dryer between each coat and again after the final coat.
2. Cut several strips of clear dichroic glass approximately 1/4" (6.4 mm) wide. From these narrow strips cut 6 pieces approximately 1 1/2" (3.8 cm) long and 12 pieces approximately 1/2" (1.3 cm) long for each snowflake that you're making. Exact widths and lengths are not critical.

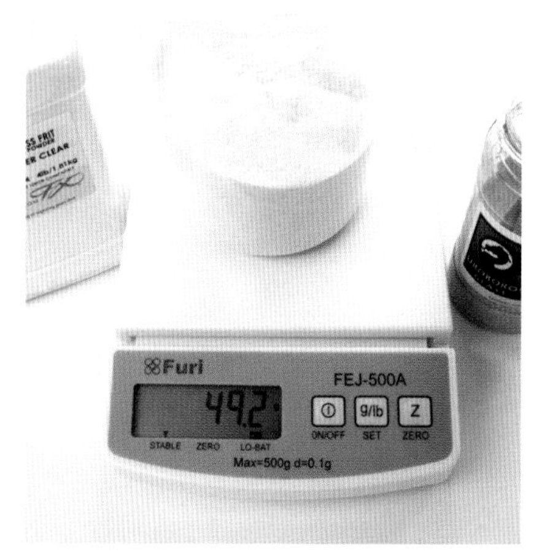


3. Place these dichroic glass pieces into the snowflake's spokes (see photo) with the dichroic-coated side down against the mold to ensure the dichroic will sparkle and glitter on the front side of the snowflake after firing.
4. Now weigh 50 grams of fine green frit for each snowflake (or any color/clear mixture of your choosing). I chose a medium green frit to match the color of a wine goblet that I already owned (see previous page). Of course, you could make your snowflakes any color you want. This would be a great time to use your color samples (see chapter 2, pages 16 to 19) to help you determine the precise color to clear mixture percentage to ensure you get the color you're looking for.
5. Use a spoon or a small funnel to evenly fill the mold cavity with 50 grams of fine frit, taking care that the dichroic strips do not shift.

### Safety Note

It is not a good idea to breathe the dust that billows up when pouring frit (actually it's a bad idea). The fine and powdered varieties in particular create a lot of dust but any size frit can be problematic. To be safe you should get into the habit of reaching for your dust mask (and put it on) before you reach for any container of frit.

| Firing Schedule for Snowflake Casting | | | | |
|---|---|---|---|---|
| Controller Segment | Ramp Rate (Per Hour) | Target Temperature | Heat Soak Hold Time | Interaction |
| Segment 1 | 300°F / 165°C | 1410°F - 1420°F 765°C - 710°C | 8 min | Observe to Confirm Final |
| Segment 2 | AFAP Down | 960°F / 515°C | 30 min | Kiln Off |
| Kiln off cool down - Do not vent - Cool to room temperature before opening | | | | |

6. Once the fine frit is added, gently tamp the frit with the back of a spoon to pack and level it out. Repeat these steps for each snowflake that you intend to fire.
7. Lay several kiln posts on their side on the kiln shelf, then position the frit filled molds on the posts and check each mold for level and stability.
8. Close the kiln and program your kiln controller according to the firing schedule for 'Snowflake Casting' at left. For more information on controller programming procedures see pages 12 & 13.

## *Creating the Plate*

1. Use a circle cutter tool (see photo at left) to create a 9" (23 cm) circle from a sheet of standard thick 1/8" (3 mm) clear iridescent glass. I like using a circle cutter for all my round plates and bowls. It improves accuracy while saving glass and time. As a bonus the outside glass breaks away from the circle easily, leaving a very clean edge.
2. Grind the edge of the circle using a 'ripple glass' edging bit (see photo below left). This specialty bit is designed to gently round off the edge of the glass to ensure the plate has a smooth and even edge after firing. Always wear safety glasses when using a glass grinder.

3. Clean the glass disc well and place it iridized side down on a prepared kiln shelf. Use a spoon to sprinkle 150 grams of clear medium frit to cover the surface of the glass then use the back of the spoon to evenly spread it around and level it out.
4. The plate blank is now ready to be fired. The first firing will tack fuse the clear frit to the surface of the base circle to give it the appearance of frosty ice. Any frit pieces that fall onto the shelf from the edge of the glass can be removed after firing. Note: The photo at right shows a setup to fire four plate blanks at once in a 22" (56 cm) semi-square kiln.
5. Close the kiln and program your kiln controller according to the firing schedule for 'Ice Tack Fuse' below right. For more information on controller programming procedures see pages 12 & 13.
6. After the plate base circle is cool, remove it from the kiln and trim the excess frit from the edge of the plate using fine wire cutters (wearing safety glasses of course). Remove as much as you can but don't worry too much about any slight jaggy areas, these edges will smooth off during slumping.

| Firing Schedule for Ice Tack Fuse | | | | |
|---|---|---|---|---|
| Controller Segment | Ramp Rate (Per Hour) | Target Temperature | Heat Soak Hold Time | Interaction |
| Segment 1 | 250°F / 139°C | 1300°F / 705°C | 10 min | Observe to Confirm Final |
| Segment 2 | AFAP - Down | 960°F / 515°C | 1 hour | Don't Vent |
| Segment 3 | 60°F / 33°C Ramp Down | 700°F / 370°C | 1 min | Kiln Off |
| Kiln off cool down - Do not vent - Cool to room temperature before opening | | | | |

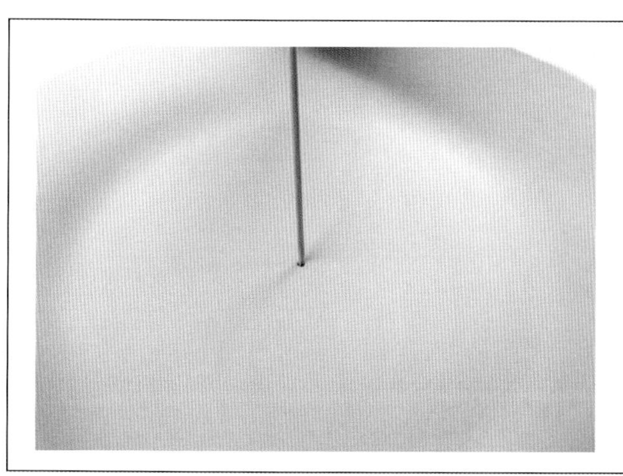

## *ProTip: A Slump Mold Needs to Breathe*

Ceramic slumping molds have vent holes drilled into the bottom of the mold to allow a place for the air to escape as the glass slumps into the mold. If any air gets trapped between the glass and the mold a large bubble will form. Therefore it is important to check the vent hole (or holes in some cases) after you have coated the mold with primer. Use a wood 'shish-kebab' skewer to poke through these vents and remove any primer that may have closed them off.

## *ProTip: Save a Step by De-Icing Your Plate*

Both plate styles shown in the photos on page 30 have the 'Ice' surface texture. The plate at the top has the snowflake tacked to the 'Ice' textured side while the lower plate has the snowflake tacked to the smooth iridescent side with the 'Ice' textured side on the bottom of the plate. You could save yourself the pre-slump 'Ice' texture firing (that we did on page 29) by leaving the 'Ice' texture off altogether (De-Icing) and simply slump and tack fuse the snowflake to the plate in one firing. Or place the plate blank on the plate slumper mold, sprinkle the ice texture frit on the plate then position the snowflake and tack fuse and slump the plate in one step as outlined below in steps 1 to 4.

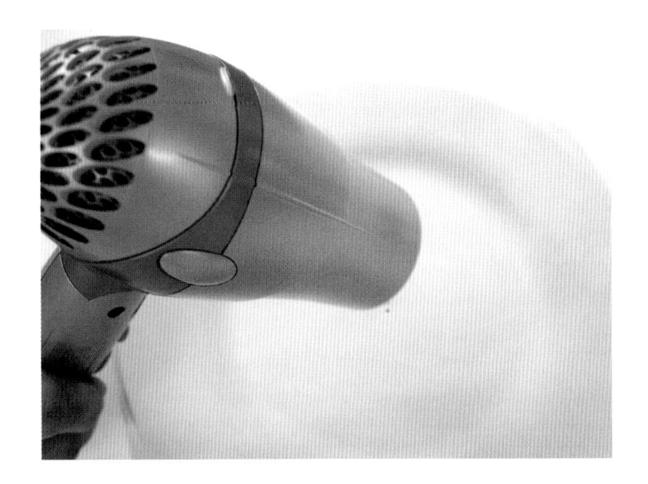

## *Slumping and Tacking the Snowflake*

1. Prepare the plate slumping mold with primer and dry mold thoroughly with the hair dryer. Use a wood skewer to open any vent holes that may be plugged with primer (see ProTip on page 33).
2. Lay three kiln posts on their side on the kiln shelf to elevate the mold during the firing, then position the plate slumper on the kiln posts and check it for level.
3. Center the plate blank on the slumper mold. You could place it with the ice textured side up, as I did for the plate shown on page 30 at top. Or place the ice textured side down (as shown at left) as I did for the lower plate on page 30. Then position a snowflake as close to the center as you can. If you want to prepare the blank at your bench then move the setup to the kiln you could use a small dab of white glue to hold the snowflake in place. I prefer to work right at the kiln positioning the blank on the mold, centering the snowflake and then let gravity hold it until it is fired.
4. Close the kiln and program your controller according to the firing schedule below for 'Tack Fusing and Slumping In One Step.'

**Firing Schedule for Tack Fusing and Slumping In One Step**

| Controller Segment | Ramp Rate (Per Hour) | Target Temperature | Heat Soak Hold Time | Interaction |
|---|---|---|---|---|
| Segment 1 | 200°F / 110°C | 1000°F / 538°C | 5 min | None |
| Segment 2 | AFAP - Up | 1275°F - 1300°F<br>750°C - 705°C | 5 to 10 minutes | Observe to Confirm Final |
| Segment 3 | AFAP - Down | 960°F / 515°C | 2 hours | Do Not Vent |
| Segment 4 | 60°F / 33°C Ramp Down | 600°F / 315°C | 1 min | Kiln Off |
| Kiln off cool down - Do not vent - Cool to room temperature before opening | | | | |

## *Snowflake Goblet*

This is a fun way to use one of the snowflake castings. It transforms an otherwise ordinary wine glass into a custom work of art. And it's easy to do so long as you have a diamond blade glass saw (if you don't have one ask your local glass shop for some help). The idea is to cut the foot base off a commercial stemware goblet and replace it with one of the snowflake castings using a few drops of ultraviolet adhesive.

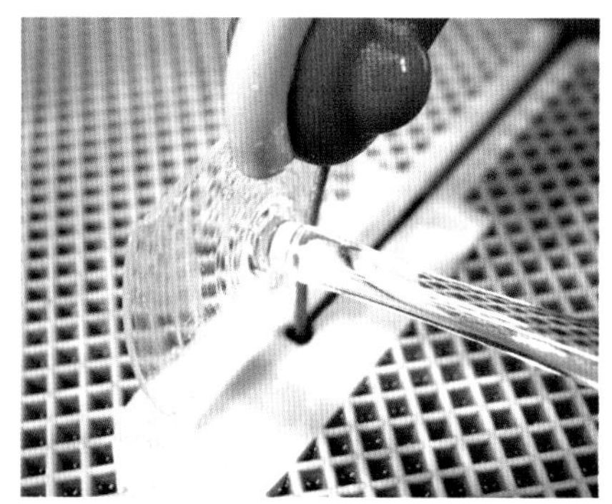

## *Here's how it's done*

1. The first step is to remove the foot base from a stemware wine glass using a diamond blade glass saw. You have to start by cutting a small piece of glass from each side of the base to allow it to fit under the blade guard of the saw. Remember to wear your safety glasses when working with the cutting saw.
2. After trimming the base sides, lay the goblet on its side, with one of the freshly cut edges down on the saw then cut through the stem as close as possible to the base. You don't want to remove too much of the stem.
3. Next smooth the cut bottom of the stem to make it flat. Do this with a traditional glass grinder or even better use a flat disc grinder if you have one available (as shown in the photo). Now place the goblet stem into the indent in the center of the snowflake to make sure everything fits. The cut bottom of the stem needs to have full contact with the snowflake and the stem has to be absolutely perpendicular.
4. Make any necessary adjustments then clean the glass and the snowflake with soap and water and dry them off. Rub isopropyl alcohol on the cut bottom of the stem and the center indent of the snowflake to prepare them for the ultraviolet adhesive.
5. Just before you apply the adhesive take a few moments to set up a propping system to stabilize the goblet while the glue is setting up. When you're ready place a few drops of ultraviolet adhesive into the center indentation of the snowflake, insert the base of the stem then prop and adjust the wine goblet until you are satisfied that it is perpendicular (you don't want the goblet leaning to one side). Finally place your ultraviolet lamp as close to the glue area as you can and leave it for at least 10 minutes or until the adhesive has fully set (be sure to read the use instructions that came with the adhesive).

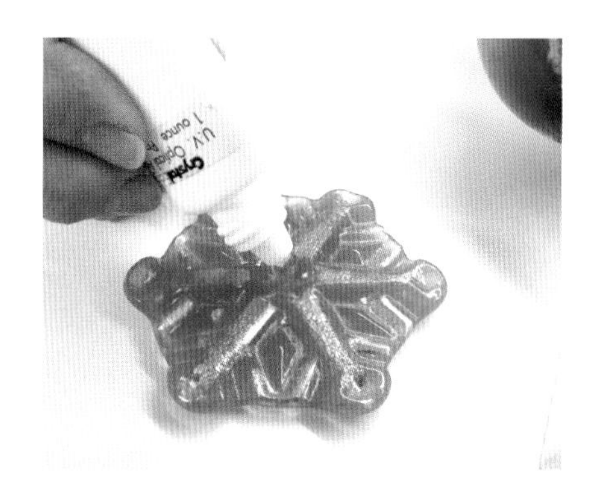

# Chapter 6 - Square Charger Plate

## Combining Multiple Components

Multiple component casting is a relatively new and exciting process that opens up a world of design possibilities. The idea is to create a number of individual components then incorporate them into one or more larger projects. This concept enables the artist to be totally in control of the color, size and design of each component individually.

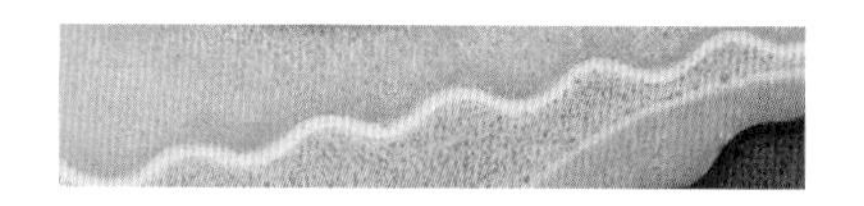

### Tools & Equipment:

- **Kiln:** Medium capacity fusing kiln with digital controller, kiln posts (assorted heights)
- **Frit Measuring & Setting:** Weigh scale, small plastic bowls, measuring pitcher (with pour spout), measuring cup, measuring spoons, small funnel, kitchen sieves & strainers (with assorted mesh sizes), applicator spoons
- **Mold Preparation:** Primo Primer™, applicator brush (soft, round), hairdryer, wood 'shish-kebab' skewer
- **Safety:** Dust mask, safety glasses, kiln gloves
- **Glass Cutting and Shaping:** Glasscutter, breaking pliers, grinder with 'ripple glass' edging bit, diamond polishing pad

### Materials:

- **Glass Supplies:** All glass for this project must have the same COE
- Fine Frit; clear, medium pink, light green, medium green, dark green
- Aqua iridized sheet - Double thick (5 mm), 11" (28 cm) square

### Forming Mold:

- 'Colour de Verre' Anemone mold
- 'Colour de Verre' Three Leaves mold
- Square plate - circle drop, slumping mold 11" to 12" (28 to 30 cm) square

## How It's Done

The project I will demonstrate in this chapter combines multiple components in two simple steps. The flowers and the leaves are cast in the first step. Then the plate will be slumped and the flowers & leaves will be tack fused to the plate in the same firing. This process only works if the slumping mold is relatively shallow - this plate is about 1" (2.5 cm). When slumping into a deeper mold it must be done in three steps as you will experience in the next chapter.

## Cast the Flowers

1. Prepare the Anemone flower mold (or mold design of your choice) with primer (see page 8 for primer instructions). The Anemone flower mold has two different flower sizes. You will need two large flowers and three medium flowers. I suggest that you make 3 large flowers since you're firing the mold anyway and use the extra flower for something else.
2. The flowers I created are translucent white with a slight blush of pink and green centers. Start by filling the center of the flowers with a combination of dark, medium and light green fine frit. Then use a spoon to sprinkle some pink fine frit into the deepest details of the flower petals. Remember to wear a dust mask when working with frit.

3. The flowers are then backfilled with clear fine frit. The large flower requires approximately 50 grams of clear fine frit and the medium flower will use approximately 45 grams of clear frit. Use a small brush around the perimeter of each flower to move some of the frit away from the outside edge of the mold to create a slight channel all the way around. Be sure to leave the frit at least 1/8" (3 mm) deep. This channel will encourage a smoother edge when the piece is fired.
4. As you can see in the photo at far right, the frit does not fill the flowers all the way. When making components that will be incorporated into another project (such as flowers and leaves) I use less frit to keep the components thinner and lighter. This will give the plate a more delicate look and a softer finish. The filled molds are now ready to be placed in the kiln.
5. Lay several kiln posts on their side on the kiln shelf and place as many filled molds as your kiln can handle. Fire the flowers using the firing schedule here.
6. The photo at right shows the final flowers still in the mold after firing and cool down.

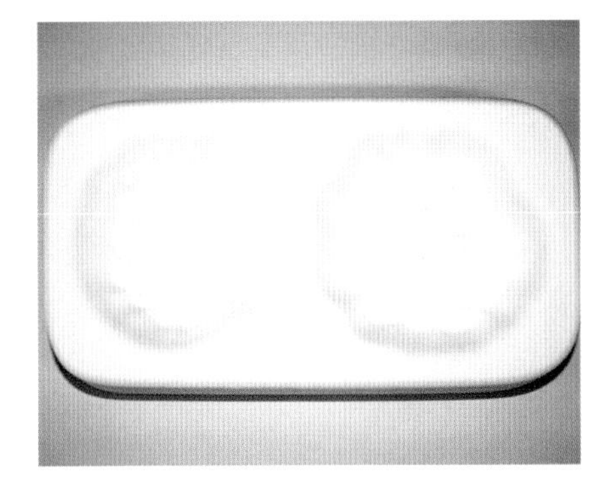

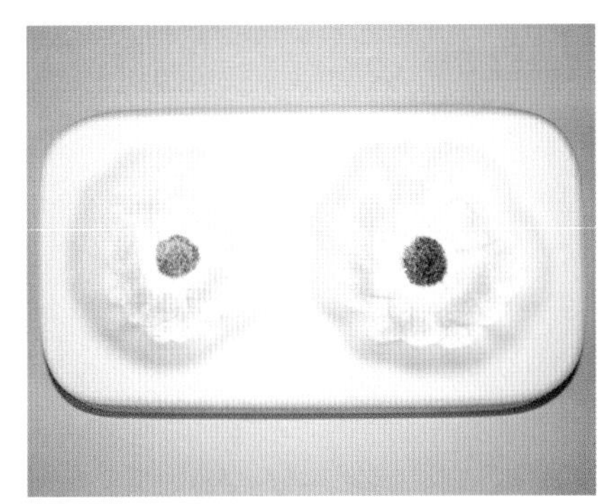

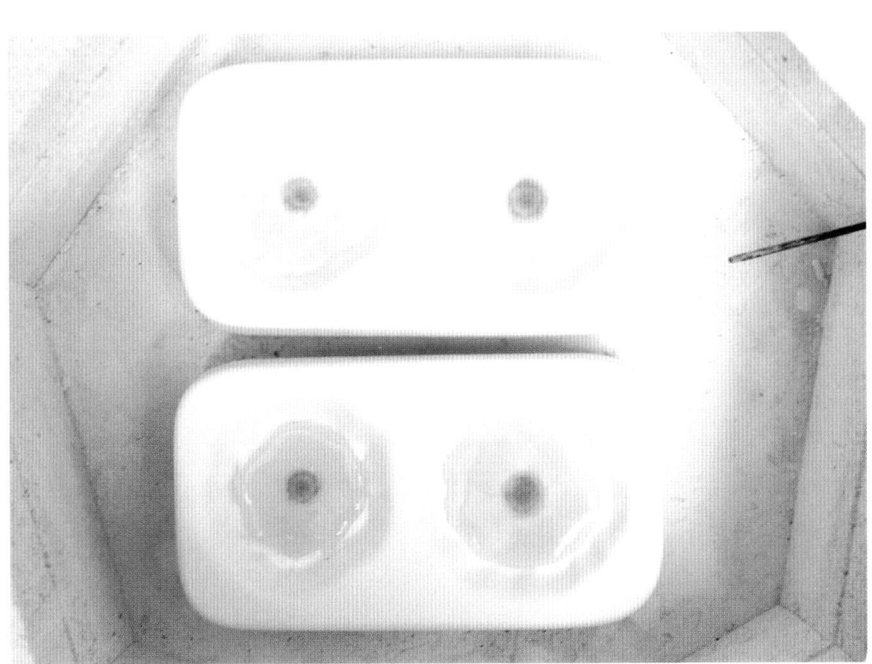

| Firing Schedule for Flowers & Leaves Casting | | | | |
|---|---|---|---|---|
| Controller Segment | Ramp Rate (Per Hour) | Target Temperature | Heat Soak Hold Time | Interaction |
| Segment 1 | 300°F / 165°C | 1410°F - 1420°F 675°C - 710°C | 8 min | Observe to Confirm Final |
| Segment 2 | AFAP Down | 960°F / 515°C | 30 min | Kiln Off |
| Kiln off cool down - Do not vent - Cool to room temperature before opening | | | | |

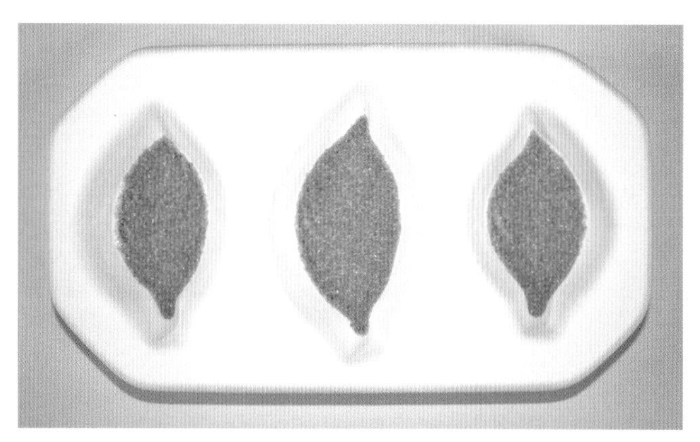

### ProTip: Thick is the Trick

Fusing glass is available in 3/16" (5 mm) thickness in clear, black and occasionally in other colors. I chose this thicker glass as the base for my charger plate because I prefer the feel and durability of a thick plate. I could have created my own thicker base glass by full fusing an 11" (28 cm) blank square using one layer of 1/8" (3 mm) glass plus a second layer of thin 1/16" (1.5 mm) glass. Of course this second layer would have to be cut into several sections to allow the air to escape when fusing. You might choose to do this additional firing if you wanted to create a special custom design for the base blank. The possibilities are endless.

## *Cast the Leaves*

1. Prepare the mold for the leaves with primer and dry well between coats.
2. Use a small kitchen sieve to sift just enough dark green fine frit to fill in the vein lines of the leaves. This will create a subtle shading effect and emphasize the veins in the leaves.
3. Next create a half & half mix of medium green and light green fine frit. Each leaf will require from 35 to 40 grams of frit so mix enough to make 6 leaves (remember to wear a dust mask!). You really only need 5 leaves for this project but since each mold makes 3, I like to fill them all and have an extra leaf to choose from. Fill each leaf cavity mold with the frit mixture - we're keeping a low fill to make these castings nice and thin. Use a small brush around the perimeter of each leaf to move some of the frit away from the outside edge of the mold.
4. Lay several posts on their side on the kiln shelf and place your filled molds on them.
5. Fire the leaves using the same firing schedule as the flowers (on page 39). The photo at left shows the final cast leaves turned face up in the mold after they were cooled.

## *Slumping the Charger Plate while Tack Fusing the Flowers & Leaves*

1. The slumping mold for this project requires an 11" (28 cm) square piece of glass. I selected an extra thick 3/16" (5 mm) aqua iridescent glass for my plate (see ProTip at left). It's important for the glass to be on square and have the edges as straight as possible. Use a glass square, a glass workshop or at the very least a metal ruler as your cutting guide.

2. Use a 'ripple glass' edging bit in your grinder to smooth and round off all edges of the plate blank.
3. Prepare the slumping mold with primer and dry it thoroughly with the hair dryer. Use a wood skewer to open any vent holes that may be plugged with primer (see ProTip on page 33).
4. Clean the glass with soap and water and place it on the mold. It is important that the glass is the same size as the mold or a little smaller. The edge of the glass should not extend beyond the mold. If the glass is larger it will slump over the outside edge of the mold and could stress both the mold and the glass causing one or both of them to crack.
5. Clean the flowers and leaves before arranging them on the square. Use a small dab of glue to keep the components from shifting when placing the project in the kiln (or assemble it right in the kiln).
6. Lay 3 kiln posts on their side on the kiln shelf and place the slumping mold in your kiln. Check it for stability and make sure the plate is square on the mold, then fire the kiln using the firing schedule here.

| Firing Schedule for Slumping & Tack Fusing Together | | | | |
|---|---|---|---|---|
| Controller Segment | Ramp Rate (Per Hour) | Target Temperature | Heat Soak Hold Time | Interaction |
| Segment 1 | 200°F / 110°C | 1000°F / 538°C | 10 min | None |
| Segment 2 | AFAP - Up | 1260°F - 1300°F<br>680°C - 705°C | 10 min | Observe to Confirm Final |
| Segment 3 | AFAP - Down | 960°F / 515°C | 3 Hours | Do Not Vent |
| Segment 4 | 60°F / 33°C Ramp Down | 800°F / 427°C | 1 min | Do Not Vent |
| Segment 5 | 100°F / 56°C Ramp Down | 600°F / 315°C | 1 min | Kiln Off |
| Kiln off cool down - Do not vent - Cool to room temperature before opening | | | | |

# Chapter 7 - Large Floral Bowl

## Full Component Project

This beautiful pink floral bowl is the largest project in this book and it also happens to be the most complicated. This bowl requires 40 to 45 cast flowers, 15 or 16 cast leaves, plus a 16" (40 cm) disc of transparent pink glass. It also requires a fair bit of patience and multiple firings... but this bowl is spectacular and it's worth every step!

### Tools & Equipment:

- **Kiln:** Minimum 20" (51 cm) diameter fusing kiln with digital controller, kiln posts
- **Frit Measuring & Setting:** Weigh scale, small plastic bowls, measuring pitcher (with pour spout), measuring cup, measuring spoons, small funnel, kitchen sieves & strainers (with assorted mesh sizes), applicator spoons
- **Mold Preparation:** Primo Primer™, applicator brush (soft, round), hairdryer, wood 'shish-kebab' skewer
- **Safety:** Dust mask, safety glasses, kiln gloves
- **Glass Cutting and Shaping:** Glasscutter, circle cutter tool, breaking pliers, glass grinder with standard bit, grinder with 'ripple glass' edging bit, diamond polishing pad

### Materials:

- **Glass Supplies:** All glass for this project must have the same COE
- Fine Frit; clear, pink, light green, medium green, dark green
- Course Frit; light green
- Pink (transparent) sheet - Std thick (3 mm) - 18" (46 cm) square or 16" (41 cm) precut disc

### Forming Molds:

- 'Colour de Verre' Floral (assorted) Molds
- 'Colour de Verre' Three Leaves mold
- 'Colour de Verre' 18" (46 cm) bowl slumper

## How It's Done

You will see that a full component project like this one requires a different approach than a single component (chapter 5, page 30) or a multiple component project (chapter 6, page 38). The Square Charger Plate in the previous chapter was a multiple component project and we were able to tack the flowers & leaves and slump the plate in a single firing. For this Full Component Project we'll first cast all the component parts, then we'll slump the bowl in a firing by itself then we'll tack the components to the bowl in an additional final firing. So let's get started.

## First Things First

The first task is to cast all the component parts. We need approximately 45 flowers and 16 leaves and that could take anywhere from as few as 3 to 10 or more firings, depending on how many flower and leaf molds you have and how many your kiln will hold. Even if you have quite a few of each mold (as I do) you are going to use each mold more than once for this project alone. Remember to clean the molds, recoat them with primer and make sure they are completely dry prior to re-firing (see pages 8-9 for mold preparation).

## *Flower Casting*

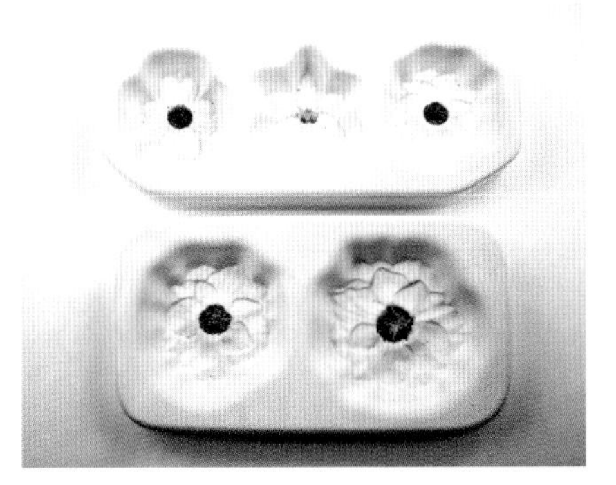

1. Use a spoon or a small funnel to fill the center of the flowers with a blend of medium and dark green frit. Don't pre-mix the frit, rather add a little of one color then some of the other to create color shading.
2. Backfill the flowers with fine pink frit. The amount varies depending on the flower design but a good rule of thumb is, 30 grams for small flowers, 40 grams for medium flowers and 50 grams for large flowers. Don't over-fill the cavity mold with frit. We're looking for a lower-level fill to keep these castings elegantly thin.
3. Use a small brush around the perimeter of each flower to move some of the frit away from the outside edge of the mold to create a slight channel all the way around. Be sure to leave the frit at least 1/8" (3 mm) deep.
4. Lay several kiln posts on their side on the kiln shelf and place as many filled molds as your kiln can handle.
5. Close the kiln and program your kiln controller according to the firing schedule for Flowers & Leaves on this page.
6. The last photo at right shows a typical full load of cast floral components after they have cooled and before the kiln is unloaded.

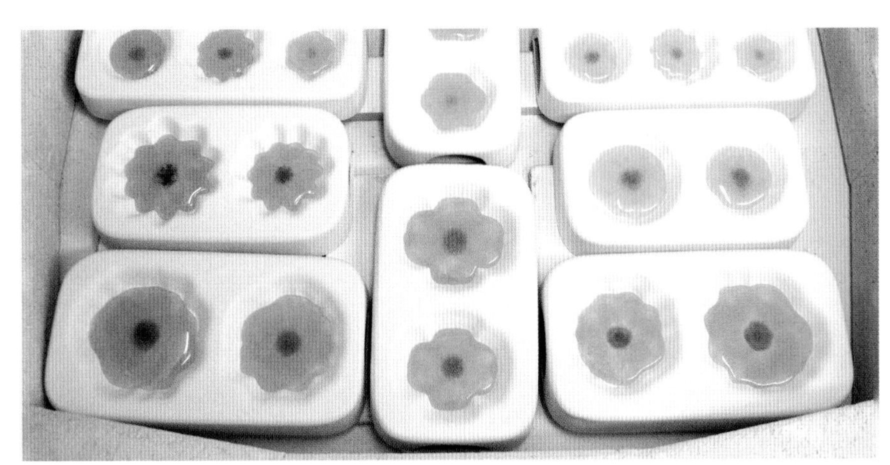

| Firing Schedule for Flowers & Leaves Casting | | | | |
|---|---|---|---|---|
| Controller Segment | Ramp Rate (Per Hour) | Target Temperature | Heat Soak Hold Time | Interaction |
| Segment 1 | 300°F / 165°C | 1400°F - 1420°F<br>660°C - 770°C | 8 to 10 minutes | Observe to Confirm Final |
| Segment 2 | AFAP Down | 960°F / 515°C | 30 min | Kiln Off |
| Kiln off cool down - Do not vent - Cool to room temperature before opening | | | | |

## Casting the Leaves

1. Prepare the mold for the leaves with primer and dry well. Use a small kitchen sieve to sift just enough dark green fine frit to fill in the vein lines of the leaves to create some visual depth.
2. Now measure 19 grams of medium green and 19 grams of light green fine frit for each leaf then back fill each cavity with a total of 38 grams (plus or minus a couple of grams is fine). You can either pre-mix the frit colors or put some light green down one side and medium green down the other side for a shaded effect. Another variation would be to mix a little dark green course frit into the light green fine frit to create a speckled texture look. This technique is particularly effective in flower centers - don't be afraid to be creative!
3. Lay several kiln posts on their side on the kiln shelf and place as many filled molds as your kiln can handle. Fire the leaves using the same firing schedule as the flowers on page 45.
4. When all flower and leaf components are finished check the edges of each one to ensure they are smooth. Use a diamond pad or your grinder with standard bit to gently remove any sharp edges.

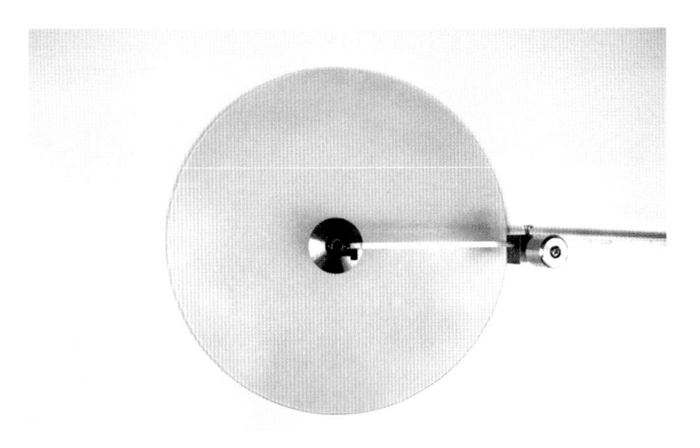

## *Creating the Slumped Bowl Base*

1. The slumping mold for this project is 18" (46 cm) in diameter however we want to make our bowl from a 16" (41 cm) circle to allow an adequate amount of space to place our leaves around the top edge of the bowl, to let them overhang the glass (but not the mold) top edge.
2. Use a circle-cutter tool for glass to score and break a 16" (41 cm) circle from standard thick 1/8" (3 mm) pink sheet glass. Or purchase a pre-cut 16" (41 cm) glass blank (be sure it has the same COE as your flowers and leaves).
3. Grind the edge of the circle using your glass grinder with the 'ripple glass' edging bit.
4. Prepare the slumping mold with primer and dry it thoroughly. Use a wood skewer to open any vent holes that may be plugged (see ProTip on page 33).
5. Lay kiln posts on the kiln shelf to elevate the mold. Clean the glass disc and center it on the mold.
6. Close the kiln and program your controller according to the firing schedule for 'Bowl Slump (Base Only)' on this page.

### *ProTip: Thin is In (this time)!*

You may have noticed that we used the thicker 3/16" (5 mm) glass for the charger plate project in chapter 6 (see ProTip on page 40) but this bowl calls for only standard thick 1/8" (3.2 mm) glass. It would seem logical that this larger 16" (41 cm) bowl should be made from glass that is at least as thick as the smaller 11" (28 cm) square charger plate. The answer is we can use thinner glass for this project because we are going to attach (by tack fusing) an additional layer of components to the inside of this bowl, creating a much thicker and stronger final product.

**Firing Schedule for Bowl Slump (Base Only)**

| Controller Segment | Ramp Rate (Per Hour) | Target Temperature | Heat Soak Hold Time | Interaction |
|---|---|---|---|---|
| Segment 1 | 150°F / 83°C | 1200°F - 1220°F<br>650°C - 660°C | 15 min | Observe to Confirm Final |
| Segment 2 | AFAP - Down | 960°F / 515°C | 2 hours | Don't Vent |
| Segment 3 | 100°F / 56°C<br>Ramp Down | 400°F / 200°C | 1 min | Kiln Off |
| Kiln off cool down - Do not vent - Cool to room temperature before opening | | | | |

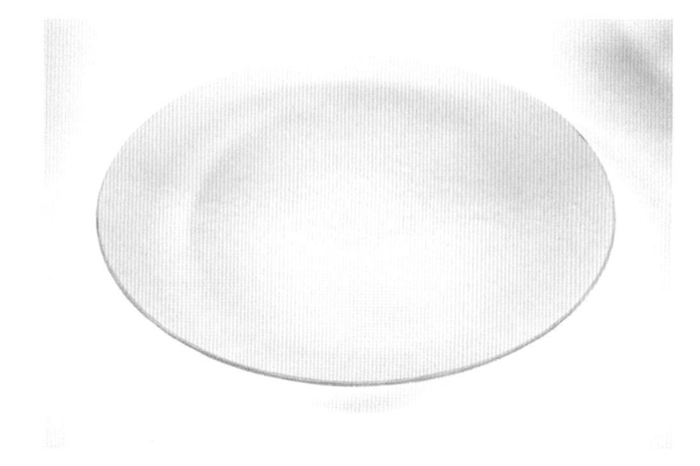

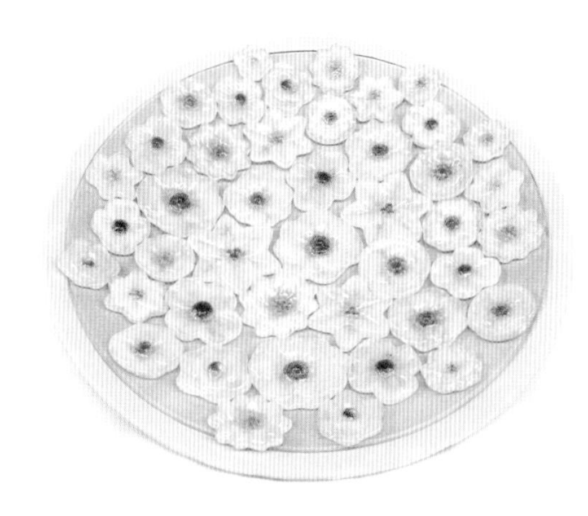

## *Assemble the Flowers & Leaves*

1. Remove the bowl base from the slump mold after it has cooled. Clean and re-coat the slumping mold with primer and remember to check the vent holes.
2. Place the now-slumped bowl base back into the re-coated slumping mold. Carefully arrange the flowers in the inside bottom of the bowl. Try to get a close fit by mixing up the sizes and rotating them until the petals mesh together. It's a good idea to use a small amount of glue on the bottom of each flower to hold them in place. When you have all flowers in position let the fabrication rest until the glue has dried.
3. The next step is to place the leaves around the top edge of the bowl. Arrange them at various angles and tuck them into spaces between the flowers. The leaves should hang out past the edge of the glass bowl but you must keep them inside the top edge of the mold. It's a good idea to secure the leaves with a little glue otherwise they have a tendency to shift when you move the assembly to your kiln. Be sure to give the glue adequate time to dry before going on to the next step.

## *Filling in the Cracks*

4. The final fabrication step is to fill the open spaces between the flowers with some light green coarse frit. This will strengthen the assembly and create a visual contrast between the flowers. Use a spoon to place enough frit in these spaces to just fill them up, be careful to keep frit off the surface of the flowers. If some frit does end up on the flowers use a small brush to sweep any pieces back into the spaces.
5. This project assembly has been quite a journey but the beautiful flower bowl is now ready for its' final firing. Lay three kiln posts on their side on the kiln shelf to elevate the mold during the firing then carefully position the mold & glass assembly on the kiln posts and check it for level and stability.
6. Close the kiln and program your controller according to the firing schedule for 'Large Floral Bowl Final' on the next page.

## *A Note About the Firing*

I mentioned in the introduction to this project that it requires multiple firings and a fair bit of patience. Well, here we are down to one last firing and congratulations are in order for getting this far! But don't let down your guard just yet - this step really requires patience. As you know, this project has dozens of pre-fired components and a large pre-slumped bowl making it a rather thick assembly. For this reason the ramp up speed, the anneal soak and ramp down speed have to be very slow. It's going to take 7 hours just to get up to the 1st segment hold temperature. Then about 2 hours to get up to tack temperature, soak it, and back down to the anneal temperature. Then anneal soak is set for 4 hours and the 3 ramp down segments will take another 16 hours. So plan on this firing taking 24 hours to complete and then you still have to wait for the final cool down (another 4 plus hours). The good news is you can set your digital controller to do all the work for you (see pages 12-13 for a discussion on digital controllers). Just set the controller and let it do its thing. Then a day and a half later you will open the kiln and be rewarded with one of the most beautiful bowls you have ever seen.

**Firing Schedule for Large Floral Bowl Final**

| Controller Segment | Ramp Rate (Per Hour) | Target Temperature | Heat Soak Hold Time | Interaction |
|---|---|---|---|---|
| Segment 1 | 150°F / 83°C | 1050°F / 566°C | 15 min | None |
| Segment 2 | AFAP - Up | 1260°F - 1275°F 682°C - 690°C | 15 min | Observe to Confirm Final |
| Segment 3 | AFAP - Down | 960°F / 515°C | 4 Hours | Do Not Vent |
| Segment 4 | 30°F / 17°C Ramp Down | 700°F / 370°C | 1 min | Do Not Vent |
| Segment 5 | 60°F / 33°C Ramp Down | 400°F / 200°C | 1 min | Do Not Vent |
| Segment 6 | 100°F / 56°C Ramp Down | 200°F / 93°C | 1 min | Kiln Off |
| Kiln off cool down - Do not vent - Cool to room temperature before opening | | | | |

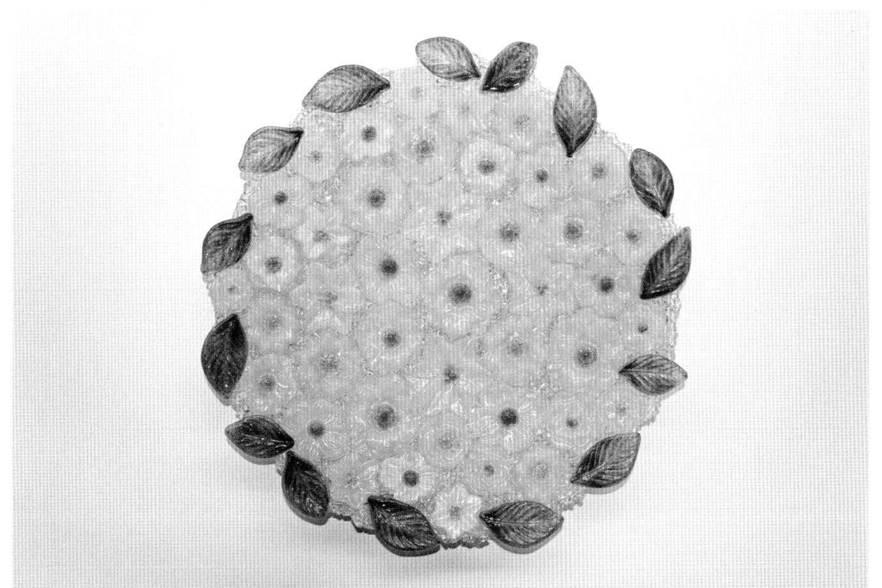

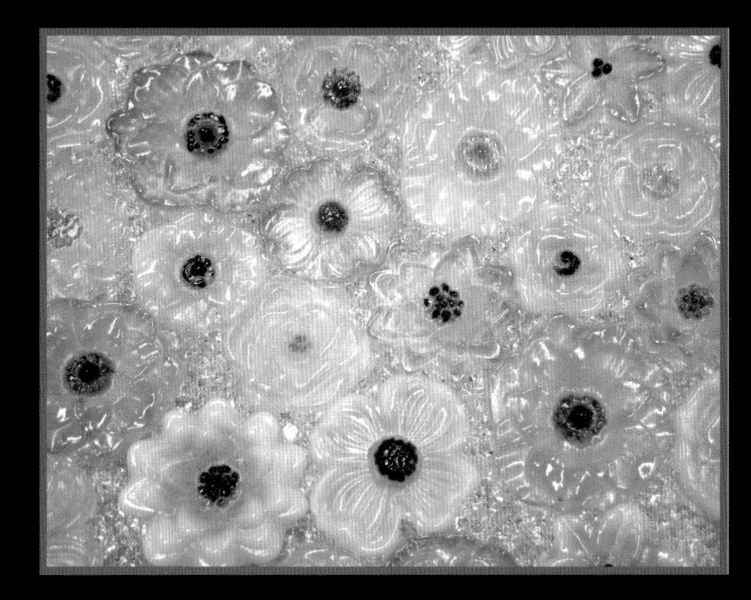

# Chapter 8 - Copper Damming System

## Barriers Can Be A Good Thing

This chapter will introduce a fun process that I developed to take advantage of the versatility of frit casting; I call it 'The Copper Damming System.'

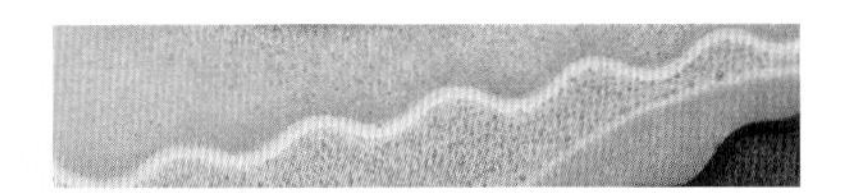

### Tools & Equipment:

- ***Kiln:*** Medium capacity fusing kiln with digital controller, kiln posts (assorted heights)
- ***Frit Measuring & Setting:*** Weigh scale, small plastic bowls, measuring pitcher (with pour spout), measuring cup, measuring spoons, small funnel, kitchen sieves & strainers (with assorted mesh sizes), applicator spoons
- ***Mold Preparation:*** Primo Primer™, applicator brush (soft, round), hairdryer, wood 'shish-kebab' skewer
- ***Pattern Preparation:*** color pencils, drawing paper metal ruler, felt tip marker
- ***Safety:*** Dust mask, safety glasses, kiln gloves, leather welding gloves
- ***Glass Cutting and Shaping:*** diamond polishing pad
- ***Metal Working Tools & Equipment:*** tin shears, fine wire cutters, alligator clips, soldering iron, solder (either 50/50 or 60/40), water-soluble flux, 2 or 3 short bungee cords

### Materials:

- ***Copper Strips:*** 1″ wide x 3′ long (2.5 cm x 92 cm) by 'Colour de Verre'
- ***Glass Supplies:*** All glass for this project must have the same COE
- Fine Frit; assorted colors
- Medium Frit; assorted colors
- Course Frit; assorted colors

### Forming Mold:

- 'Colour de Verre' disc former 10″ (25 cm)
- 'Colour de Verre' Plate slumper mold, for 10″ to 12″ plate (25 to 30 cm)

## Glass Casting in the Disc Fuser Mold

I'll show you how to design and create an original copper template that you can use to shape intricate patterns in the frit and then repeat that design when you're working on a series. This is particularly useful when you want to cast a coordinated set of plates or when you have an idea for a custom design shape (a business logo or trademark for instance) that you want to use in a casting.

In the next three chapters we will be working with the Colour de Verre 10" (25.5 cm) disc fuser mold. This form was created especially for artists who like to create original designs. You will soon find that the disc fuser is so versatile you can cast many different style plates, bowls and sculptures from just this one mold.

## *How It's Done*

**1**. I wanted a simple yet elegant design for a set of dinnerware. I created a few quick sketches with wavy lines across a circle until I came up with something that I liked. Then I used color pencils to shade my design to help me visualize my concept. I decided that my first plate would be white with a blue wave design and the other plates in the set would also be white but have a different color in the wave.

**2**. Use a drawing compass to make a 10" (25 cm) circle then create your design within the circle. You will find 6 other design possibilities scattered throughout this chapter to give you some ideas of what can be accomplished. When you have your full-size drawing completed the way you want it, trace it with a black marker.

**3**. Prepare the 10" (25 cm) disc former using primer in the usual way, drying with a hairdryer between coats and thoroughly after the last coat.

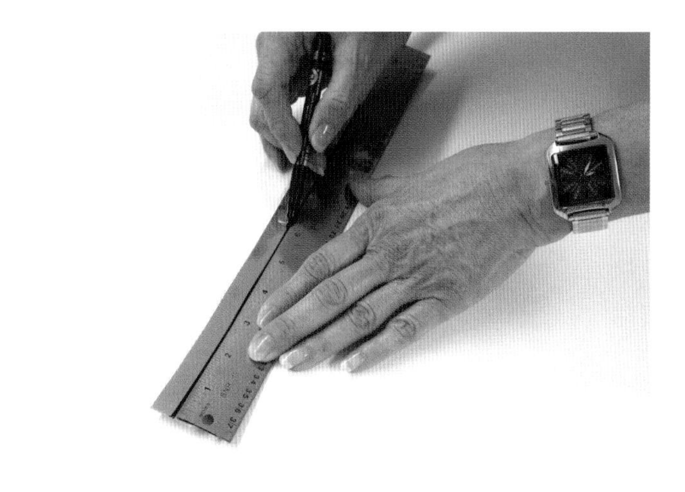

**4**. The copper strips (manufactured by Colour de Verre) are 1" wide x 3' long (2.5 cm x 92 cm). The first thing you need to do is draw a dividing line lengthwise down the middle of each strip, using a permanent marker. Turn the strip over and repeat on the opposite side. This mark will be used as the fill line when adding frit to the assembly.

**5**. Use tin shears to cut a length of the copper strip 33" (84 cm) long. This copper is flexible enough to be formed using just your hands. However you should wear safety glasses whenever you're cutting, shaping and soldering metal.

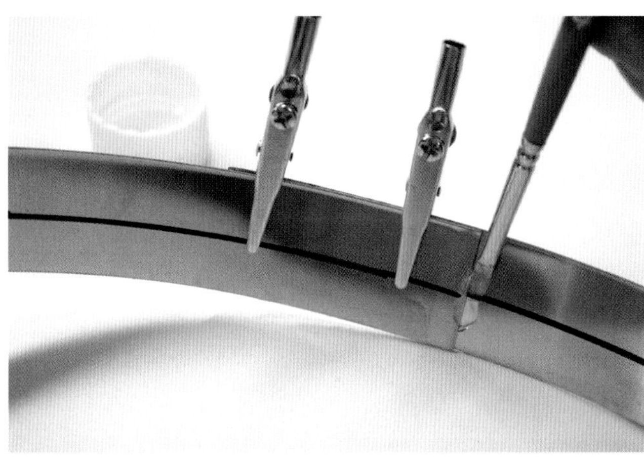

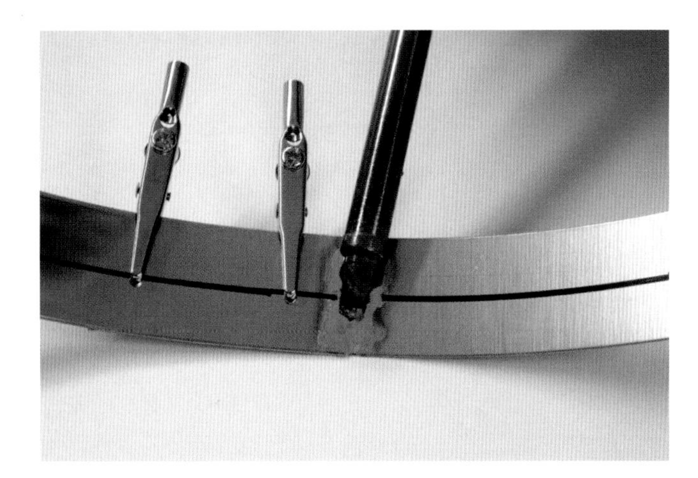

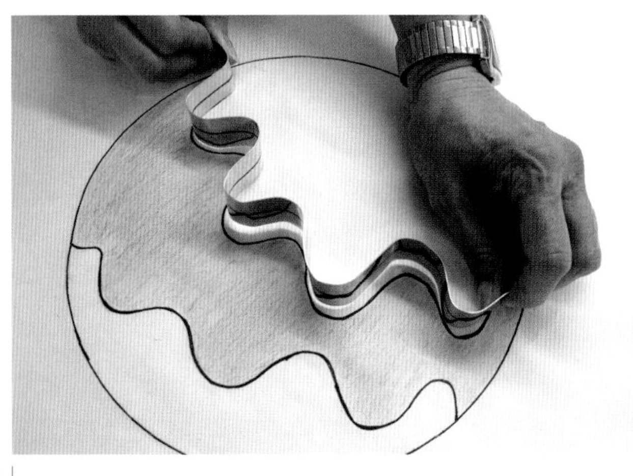

**6**. Gently bend the strip to fit around the perimeter circle on your drawing. The overlap should be approximately 1 1/2" to 2" (3.8 to 5 cm). Trim it if necessary then secure the overlapped area with a couple of alligator clips. Place it back on your drawing to check again that it fits your pattern.

**7**. You are now ready to solder the copper seam on the inside of the circle. I like to wear a lightweight welding glove when soldering copper strip because it gets hot quickly (copper is a excellent conductor of heat) and you'll want to hold the strip steady as you solder. Apply a little water-soluble flux to the seam that is to be soldered.

**8**. Get the soldering iron hot then place the tip of the iron directly on the overlapped copper seam and give it some time to get hot. Now touch the end of the solder wire to the copper seam. The solder should melt and be drawn into the overlapped seam. If it doesn't melt right away you need to let the copper heat up a little more and try again (did you remember to flux it?). Flux and solder the outside seam as well, then let the copper circle cool.

**9**. Now shape the inside design strips. In my design I will bend the strips to follow the wavy lines on my design drawing. Trim the inside strips allowing them to extend 1/2" (1.3 cm) beyond the circle. Now use pliers to bend the 1/2" (1.3 cm) extensions to create tabs that can be soldered to the inside of the circle.

*This dove motif is an alternate design for the copper damming system. See pages 56, 57 & 58 for more alternates.*

**10**. Use the alligator clips to temporarily attach the first copper design strip to the outer copper ring. Check again to make sure it follows your design then solder it to the outer ring. Now shape and fit the next strip in your design and solder it to the assembly. Continue to shape, fit and solder each strip until your design is complete. Finally clean the flux off all the seams with soap and water (be careful, the copper edges can be sharp) but take care that you don't clean off the marker line.

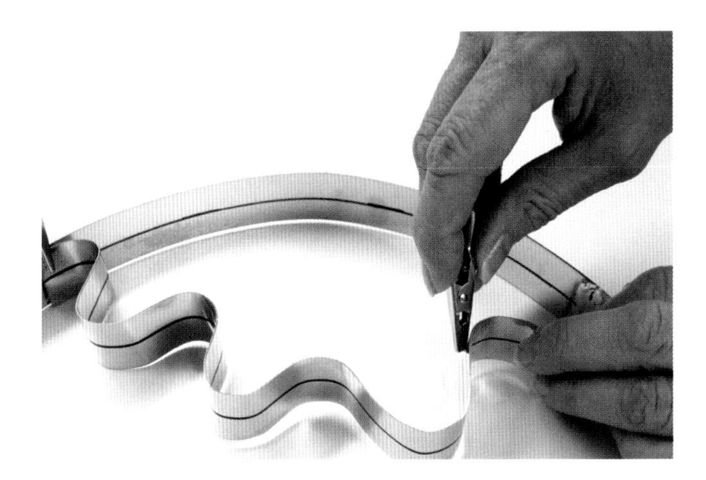

**11**. Place the finished copper template in the disc fuser mold. You will notice that the copper ring does not fit flat against the inner wall of the mold. The mold is designed with tapered wall that will allow the glass to release from the mold after the plate has been cast. We will fill this outer area with frit at the end to complete the design.

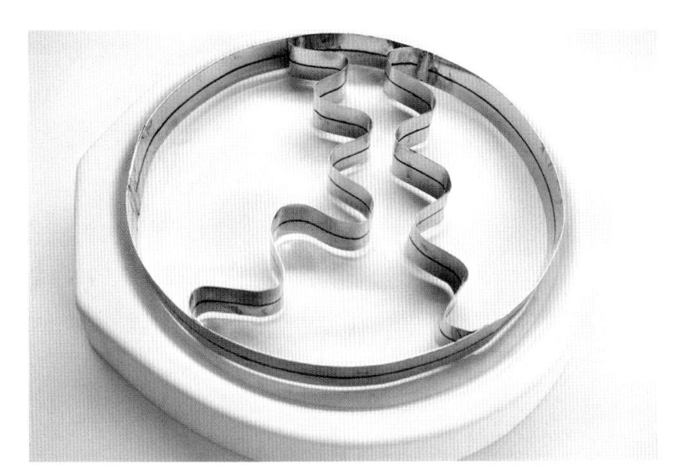

**12**. Fasten 2 short bungee cords stretched across the top of the copper template to hold it securely to the mold floor while filling the sections with frit. I like to place the mold on a 'lazy-susan' turntable so I can easily turn it while filling with frit.

**13**. One final check before filling the mold, the template should be sitting flat against the bottom of the mold. If there are any gaps between the copper and the mold fill these gaps with clear fine frit to prevent the colors from mixing under the dams.

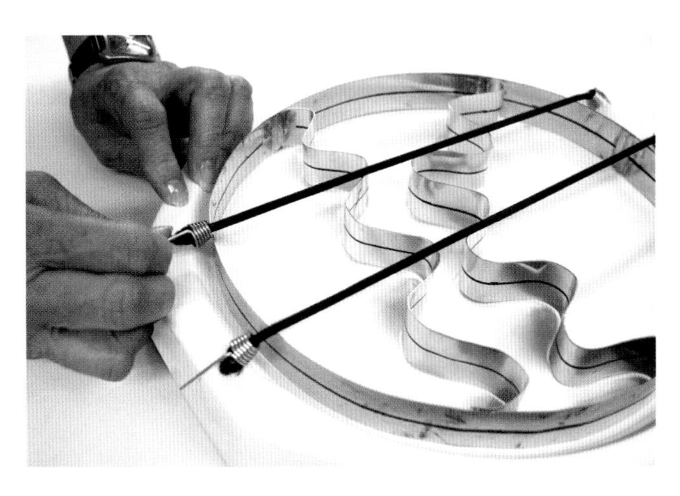

**14**. Now we'll prepare the frit for our design. This 10" (25 cm) disc will use about 900 grams of frit total to fill it up to the guideline that you put on the copper in the first step. I will use 600 grams of clear fine frit (that will appear translucent white after firing) and 300 grams of blue fine frit for my design. You will of course use the colors that are appropriate for your design. It's not critical to weigh the frit for this copper-damming project. The important thing is to fill the template up to the fill guideline only - do not overfill it past this line.

**15**. OK now we're ready to fill the mold. My design has three sections (your design may have more). I will fill the two outside sections with clear fine frit and the inside wave with blue fine frit. When you have filled all template sections to the fill line, use the back of a spoon to pack the frit down so that it is even, level and tight.

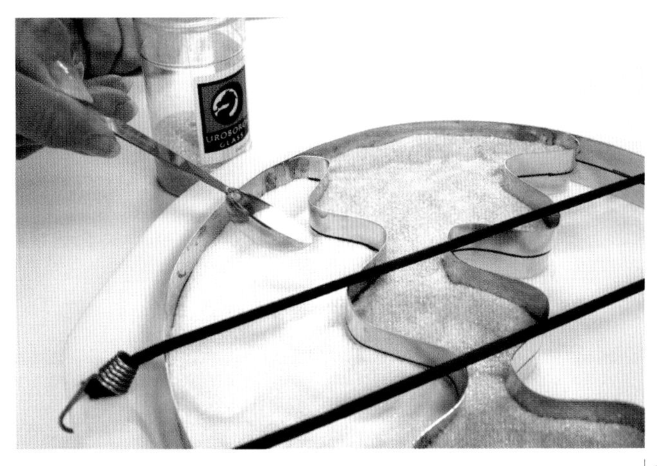

**16**. Now fill the space around the outside edge - between the copper circle and the inside wall of the mold. I like to use a small tapered spoon to fill this section up to the fill line with frit. You'll notice that I matched the frit color in this outside space with the color that is on the inside of the ring. I wanted the color to extend all the way to the outside edge of my plate, however you could put a contrasting color in this outside space (black for instance) to create a black frame around the perimeter of the plate. Fill this area with frit up to the fill line and pack it down to make it level and tight.

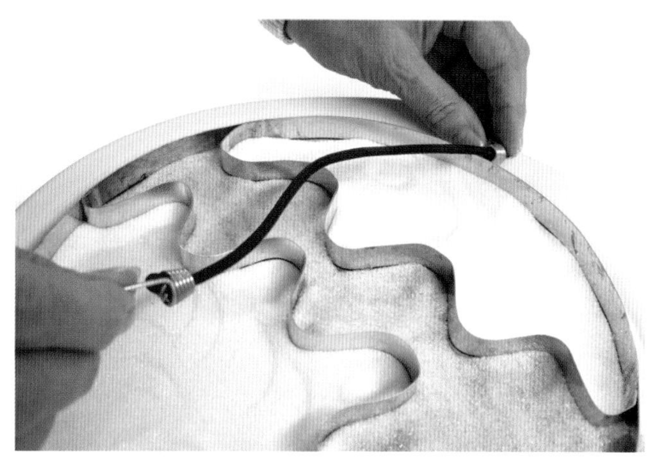

**17**. Now the real magic happens. Remove both bungee cords. Grasp the copper ring with both hands and slowly, carefully lift the copper template straight up. Voila your frit design is born.

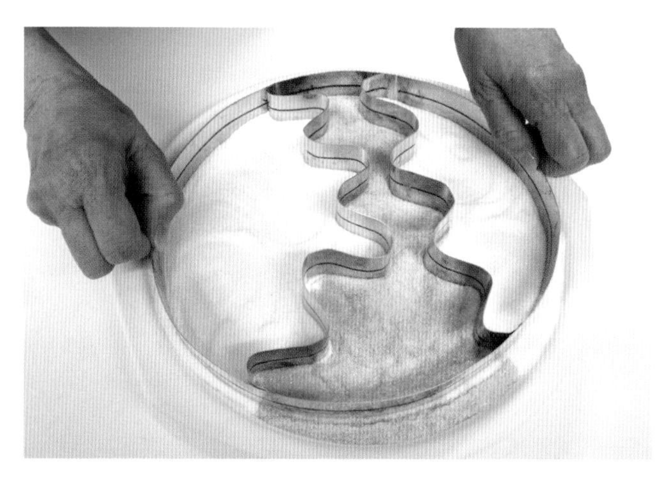

**18**. This next step is very important. If you look carefully you will see a slight space at the seams where the frit colors meet - this is the space left by the copper template. Use your finger to press down along these seams to bring the frit together tightly. This is a very important step - if this is not done the glass will separate along these seams when it is heated. This is especially true when a dark color and a light color are next to each other. The darker color will absorb the heat a little quicker, causing it to shrink and pull away, opening a slit in the glass. Sometimes I'll even go one step further - I turn a frit jar upside down and use the top of the lid to tamp down and tightly pack the frit.

*The palm tree above, plus the river and the wave motif on the next page, are alternate designs that would work very well with this copper damming system.*

19. Lay kiln posts on the shelf to elevate the mold. Close the kiln and program your controller according to the firing schedule for 'Disc Casting.'

## *Slump the Plate*

1. The flat disc is now ready to take shape on the slumping mold. Prime the slumping mold and check the vent holes.
2. Check the perimeter edge of your disc for sharp points and use a diamond polishing pad to smooth them off. If you touched the top surface and left fingerprints, you'll need to clean and dry the disc before positioning it on the mold.
3. Lay kiln posts on the kiln shelf to elevate the mold. Close the kiln and program your controller according to the firing schedule for 'Cast Plate Slumping.'
4. Be sure to wait until the kiln has cooled completely then open it to reveal your first plate. Now you can go ahead and reuse your copper template as many times as you want, to cast the rest of the plates in your dinnerware set.

**Firing Schedule for Disc Casting**

| Controller Segment | Ramp Rate (Per Hour) | Target Temperature | Heat Soak Hold Time | Interaction |
|---|---|---|---|---|
| Segment 1 | 250°F / 139°C | 1200°F / 650°C | 20 min | None |
| Segment 2 | AFAP - Up | 1420°F - 1440°F 770°C - 782°C | 20 to 30 minutes | Observe to Confirm Final |
| Segment 3 | AFAP - Down | 960°F / 515°C | 2 Hours | Do Not Vent |
| Segment 4 | 60°F / 33°C Ramp Down | 700°F / 370°C | 1 min | Kiln Off |
| Kiln off cool down - Do not vent - Cool to room temperature before opening | | | | |

**Firing Schedule for Cast Plate Slumping**

| Controller Segment | Ramp Rate (Per Hour) | Target Temperature | Heat Soak Hold Time | Interaction |
|---|---|---|---|---|
| Segment 1 | 200°F / 111°C | 1200°F / 650°C | 10 to 15 minutes | Observe to Confirm Final |
| Segment 2 | AFAP - Down | 960°F / 515°C | 2 Hours | Don't Vent |
| Segment 3 | 60°F / 33°C Ramp Down | 700°F / 370°C | 1 min | Kiln Off |
| Kiln off cool down - Do not vent - Cool to room temperature before opening | | | | |

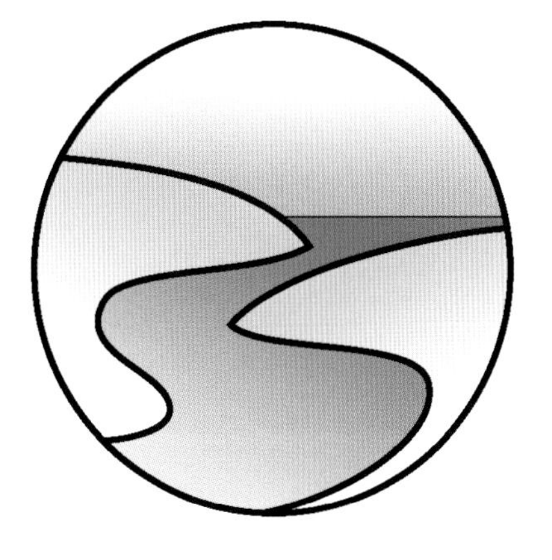

I have a cute little floral template that I made with a short length of copper strip for a previous project. I used this template to enhance my simple wave design with a purple flower (see photo at right).

As you work with this copper damming system you will eventually build an inventory of components that you can use to create an endless variety of designs. In fact you don't even have to use the 10" (25 cm) copper ring as we did in this project. You could place 'standalone' components (i.e. the wine glasses in the sketch below) directly into the disc former mold then secure it/them with bungee cords. This is an advanced technique because the components have a serious tendency to shift and move as you add the frit. It's a very delicate operation that requires patience - but the results can be rewarding.

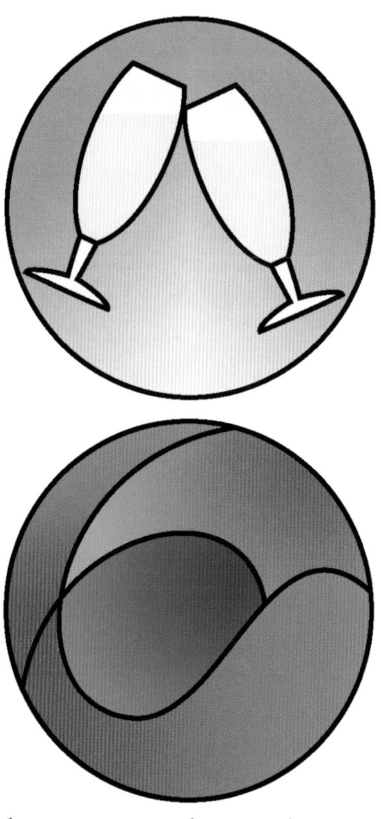

*Above, two more alternate designs.*

*Here is yet another variation. This flat disc became a great sculptural piece by tack fusing a cast dragonfly and mounting it on a metal stand (available at most glass supply centers). This decorative piece of art would be a lovely addition to any sunroom!*

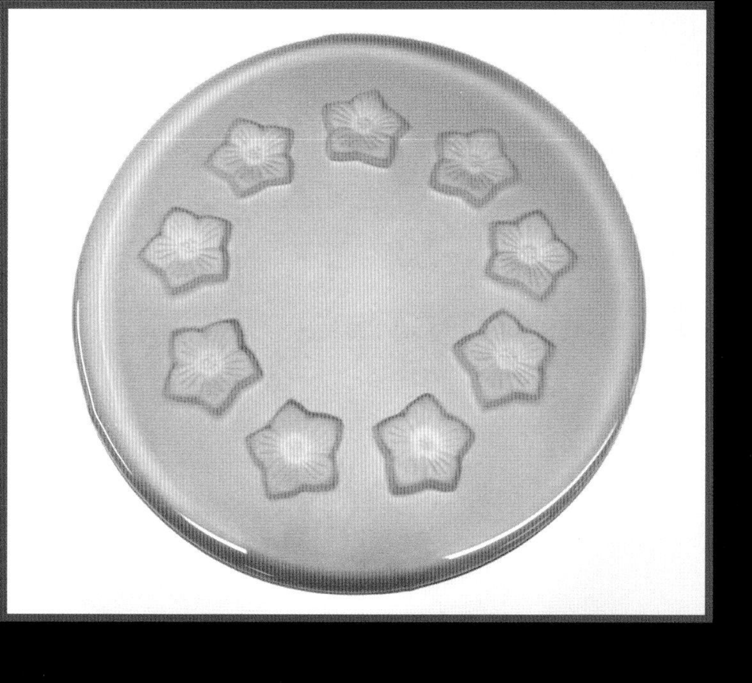

# Chapter 9 - Glass Dams

## *The Dam is Part of the Design*

In the last chapter we worked with copper strips to create a reusable dam with a repeatable pattern. In this chapter we will build our frit dams using glass strips to create one of a kind art pieces. Unlike the copper strips that we removed before the firing, these glass dams will not be removed and will be fused into the plate to become a central part of the design. You can use this process to create a texture 'tack-fuse' effect or a full melt 'smooth-fuse' project.

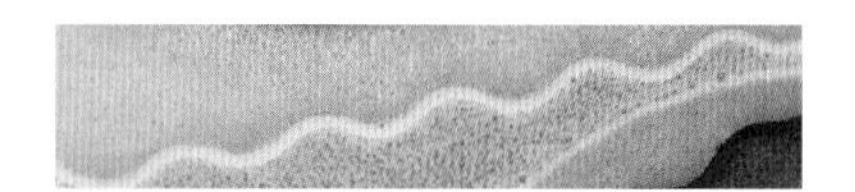

### *Tools & Equipment:*

- ***Kiln:*** Medium capacity fusing kiln with digital controller, kiln posts (assorted heights)
- ***Frit Measuring & Setting:*** measuring pitcher (with pour spout), applicator spoons, small funnel
- ***Mold Preparation:*** Primo Primer™, applicator brush (soft, round), hairdryer
- ***Pattern Preparation:*** color pencils, drawing paper metal ruler, felt tip marker
- ***Safety:*** Dust mask, safety glasses, kiln gloves
- ***Glass Cutting and Shaping:*** Glasscutter, breaking pliers, glass grinder with standard bit, diamond polishing pad

### *Materials:*

- ***Glass Supplies:*** All glass for this project must have the same COE

- Fine Frit; assorted colors
- Medium Frit; assorted colors
- Course Frit; assorted colors
- Glass sheets - Std thick (3 mm), assorted colors

### *Forming Mold:*

- 'Colour de Verre' disc former 10" (25 cm)
- Plate slumping mold, for 10" to 12" plate (25 to 30 cm)
- a selection of molds with curves, waves and/or zigzag shapes

## *Make a Variety of Dam Strips*

We'll use the same 10" (25 cm) disc fuser mold that we used in the previous chapter to create both a texture fuse and a full fuse plate. The fabrication steps are exactly the same for both of these plates, but as you would expect the firing schedules will be different. You will see that the results are unique and quite striking!

**1.** The first thing we need to do is create a variety of glass dams. These dams are going to be fused directly into our plate so they must have the same COE as the frit we plan to use. We'll cut some 3/8" (1 cm) wide glass strips in a variety of colors, then slump those strips on a selection of molds to create curves, waves and zigzag elements.

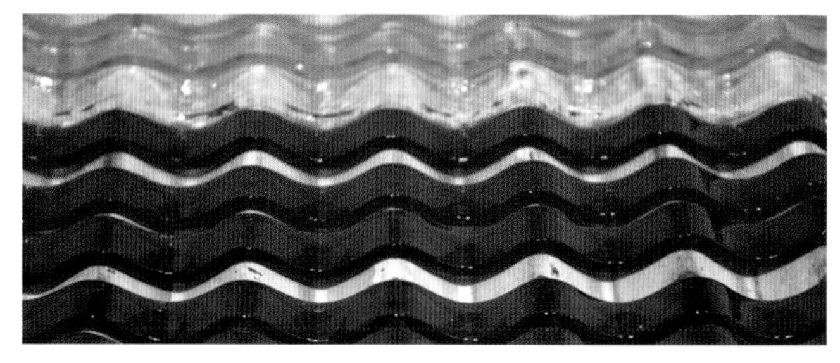

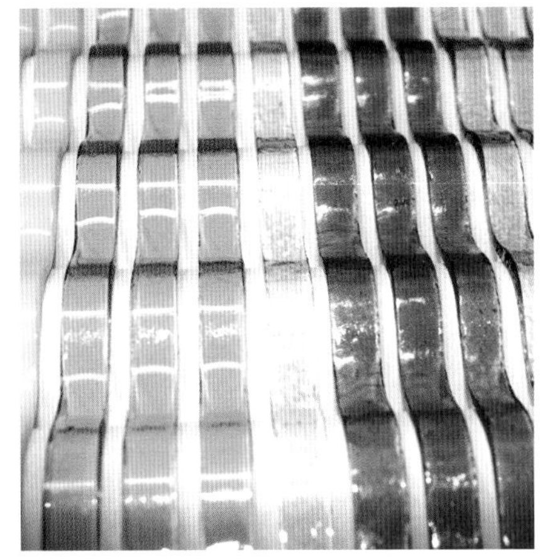

2. The slumping molds can be ceramic, stainless steel or fiberboard. We're looking for molds with interesting and undulating curves to give us some great shapes to work with. Prepare the molds in the usual way (depending on the mold material) then place them in your kiln.
3. Each plate will need from 6 to 10 dams strips but I like to have an assortment of colors and shapes to choose from so I usually slump 40 to 50 at once. Cut a variety of colored glass strips 3/8" (1 cm) wide by 10" to 12" (25 to 30 cm) long.

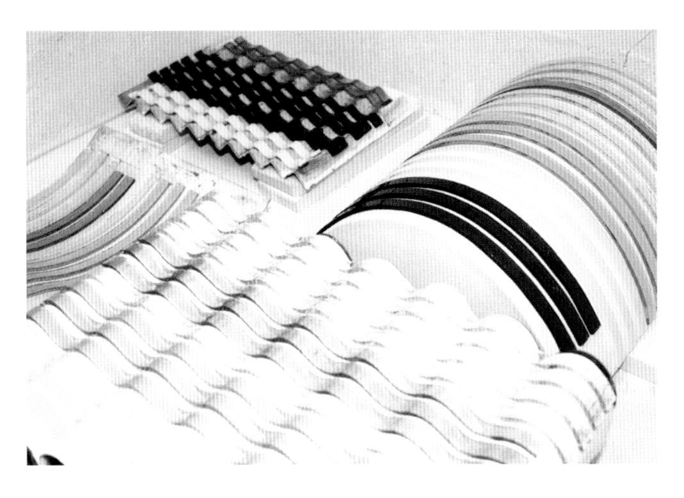

4. Clean and dry these glass strips then arrange them on the slumping molds in the kiln, leaving approximately 3/16" (5 mm) space between each strip.
5. Close the kiln and program your controller according to the firing schedule for 'Dam-strip Slumping.'

**Firing Schedule for Dam-strip Slumping**

| Controller Segment | Ramp Rate (Per Hour) | Target Temperature | Heat Soak Hold Time | Interaction |
|---|---|---|---|---|
| Segment 1 | 400°F / 222°C | 1200°F - 1220°F<br>650°C - 660°C | 15 min | Observe to Confirm Final |
| Segment 2 | AFAP Down | 960°F / 515°C | 15 min | Kiln Off |
| Kiln off cool down - Do not vent - Cool to room temperature before opening | | | | |

## *Now the Real Fun Begins!*

1. Prepare the 10" (25 cm) disc former using primer in the usual way, drying with a hairdryer between coats and thoroughly after the last coat. For this project I am going to make 2 glass-dam discs at the same time (fortunately I have 2 disc fuser molds). One of them will be 'texture' fused, meaning it will be heated only until the glass and frit particles tack together, but before they fully melt and the surface becomes smooth. The other disc will be taken to full-fuse, until the frit and glass particles have fully combined and the surface has smoothed over.

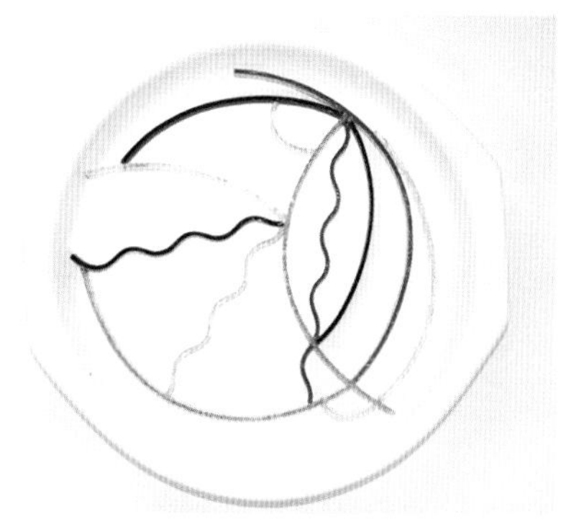

2. Creatively arrange a few glass strips in the disc fuser mold. You could just create a design on the fly or cut the strips to follow a predetermined design. The only rules are the strips have to be standing on their side and they can't stack on top of one another.
3. The dams can (and will) shift when the frit is added. The best way to reduce this possibility is to secure the assembly with a small amount of glue wherever the dam-strips touch one another. Give the glue sufficient time to cure before filling.
4. Fill each section with frit. Depending on frit size and the amount needed to fill a section, you could use a measuring pitcher with a pour spout, a spoon, a funnel, a plastic applicator bottle or any other frit applicator that you like. The frit needs to be loaded until it is mounded slightly higher than the glass dams in each section. This 'mounding up' is really important. I like to fill the spaces to level, then tamp the frit down as tightly as possible, then add another layer of frit to bring each section above the top of the glass dams, then tamp it again. Finally I use a small brush to remove any stray frit from the top of the dams.

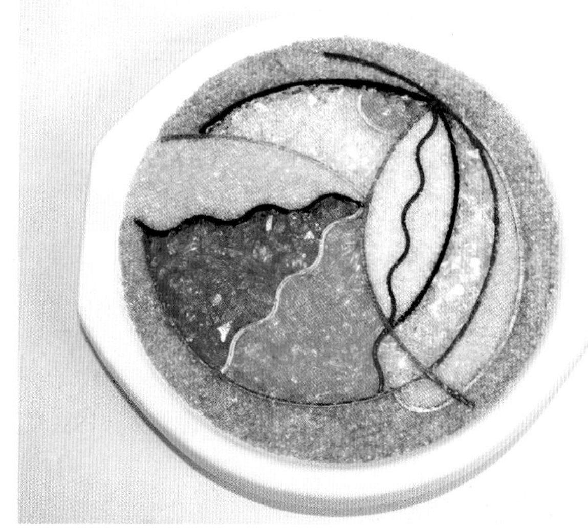

5. As I mentioned in the introduction to this project, one of the plates will be texture fused (sometimes called tack fused) meaning the frit will not be heated to the point where it has melted smooth. I wanted to really emphasize the surface texture on one of the plates, so I choose medium and coarse frit for my fill. By the way, you don't have to fill each individual section with all the same color frit. You could fill one end of a section with one color and the other end with a contrasting color then blend these 2 colors together in the middle - to produce a color gradation.

6. The other plate will be taken to full fuse temperature and that means the surface will be more or less smooth. I used fine and medium frit only to fill this plate. I don't recommend mixing the smaller size frits (powder, fine & medium) with the larger size frits (coarse & mosaic) within the same full fuse project. Smaller sized frit requires less soak time than larger sized frit and this difference could create an uneven firing. One final trick that I like to do for these full fuse projects is to place a thin layer of fine clear over the entire plate - even covering the dams. This will add depth and sheen to the surface giving it a professional touch.

7. When your mold is ready, place it in the kiln and set up the firing using the schedule that applies to your project (texture fuse or full fuse).

**Firing Schedule for 'Texture Fuse' Glass Dam Disc**

| Controller Segment | Ramp Rate (Per Hour) | Target Temperature | Heat Soak Hold Time | Interaction |
|---|---|---|---|---|
| Segment 1 | 250°F / 139°C | 1280°F - 1300°F 690°C - 705°C | 15 min | Observe to Confirm Final |
| Segment 2 | AFAP - Down | 960°F / 515°C | 2 Hours | Do Not Vent |
| Segment 3 | 60°F / 33°C Ramp Down | 700°F / 370°C | 1 min | Do Not Vent |
| Segment 4 | 100°F / 56°C Ramp Down | 500°F / 260°C | 1 min | Kiln Off |
| Kiln off cool down - Do not vent - Cool to room temperature before opening | | | | |

**Firing Schedule for 'Full Fuse' Glass Dam Disc**

| Controller Segment | Ramp Rate (Per Hour) | Target Temperature | Heat Soak Hold Time | Interaction |
|---|---|---|---|---|
| Segment 1 | 250°F / 139°C | 1200°F / 650°C | 20 min | None |
| Segment 2 | AFAP - Up | 1420°F / 770°C | 25 to 35 minutes | Observe to Confirm Final |
| Segment 3 | AFAP - Down | 960°F / 515°C | 2 Hours | Do Not Vent |
| Segment 4 | 60°F / 33°C Ramp Down | 700°F / 370°C | 1 min | Do Not Vent |
| Segment 5 | 100°F / 56°C Ramp Down | 500°F / 260°C | 1 min | Kiln Off |
| Kiln off cool down - Do not vent - Cool to room temperature before opening | | | | |

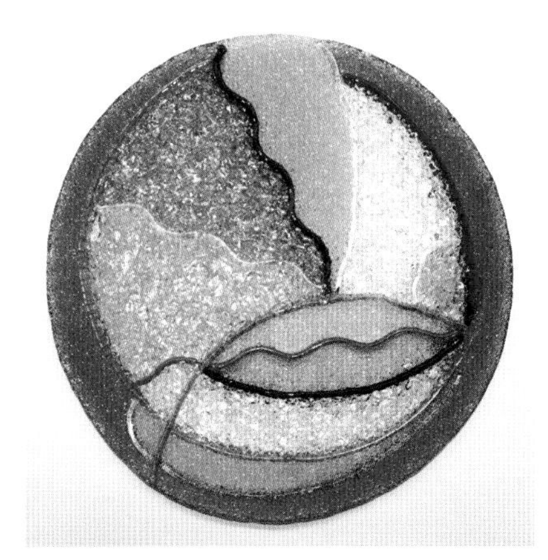

*The plate on the left is the full-fuse disc while the texture-fuse style is on the right. When your fused disc is finished you could mount it on a metal stand (as shown on page 59) or you could slump it into a plate or bowl mold (as I did for the plate above left). However, there is a limitation to the degree that you can slump one of the texture fused discs, the frit bond is somewhat delicate and can separate if you try to slump it deeper than a very shallow plate.*

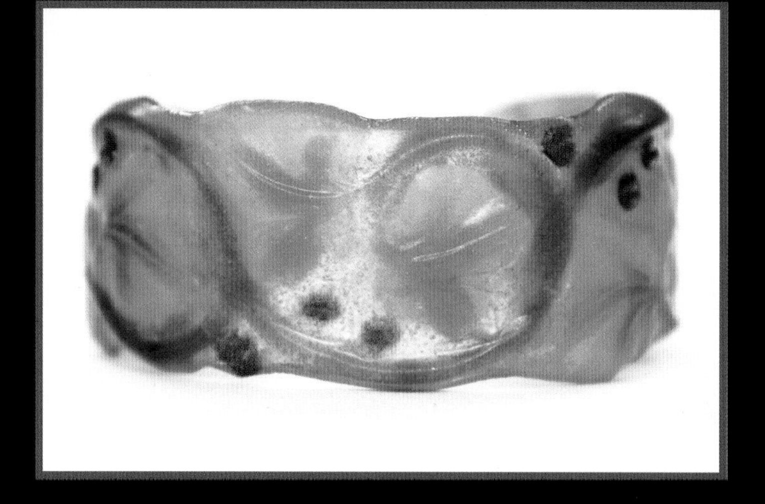

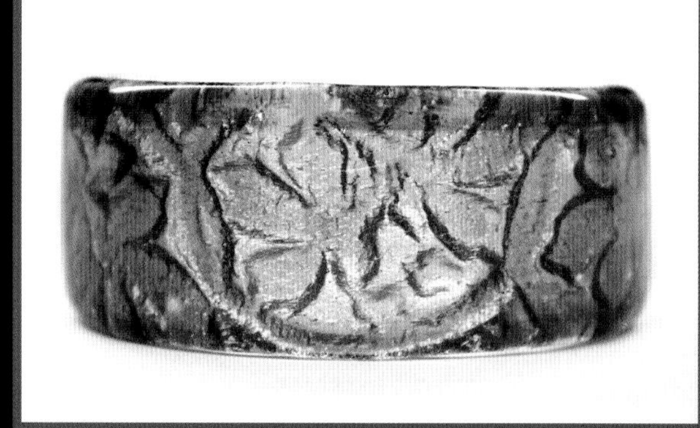

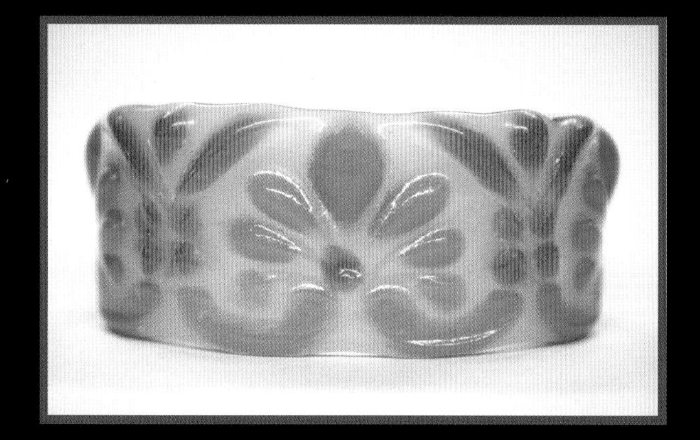

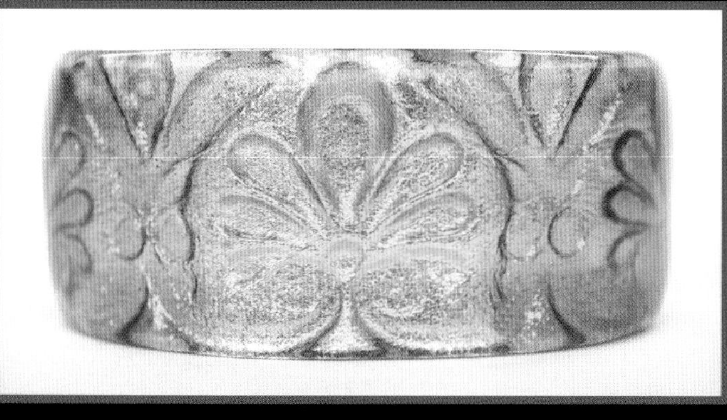

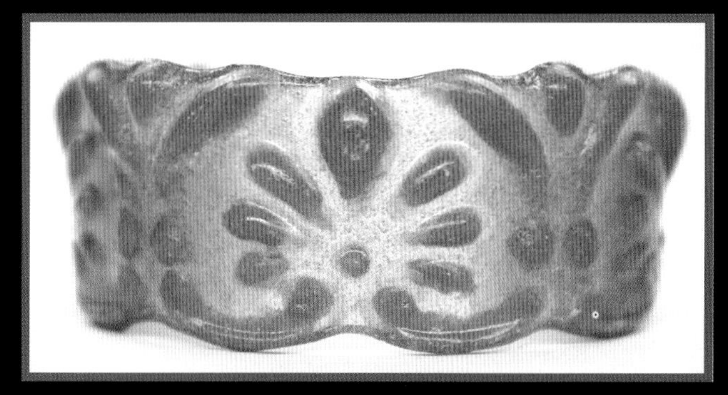

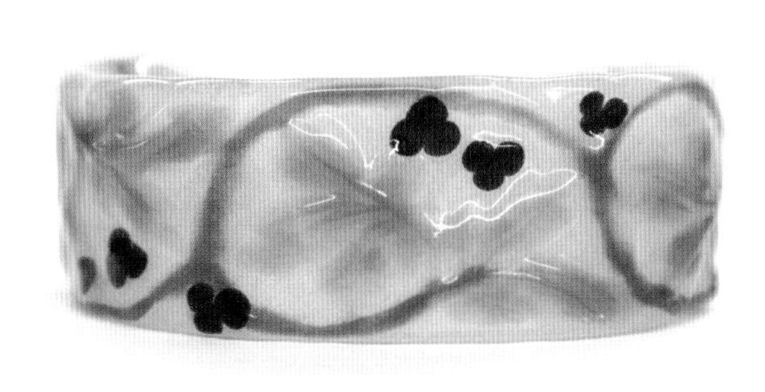

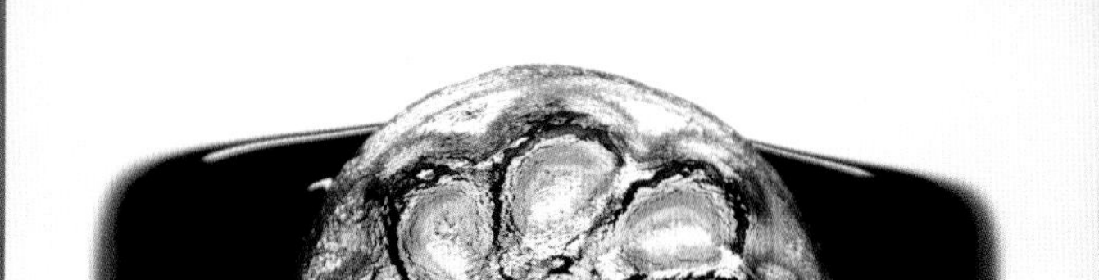

# Chapter 10 - Billet Casting

## *Embedding a Design in Thick Glass*

For this project we are going to create a thick cast plate with a design that appears to be floating within the glass. The floating design is accomplished by casting a billet of glass over a composition of plaster forms. When the billet plate has cooled the plaster forms are removed to reveal the negative space in the bottom of the casting that produces the effect. A billet is a thick slab of glass that is approximately 6" x 9" x 3/4" (15 x 23 x 2 cm), formulated especially for glass casting with a very low bubble-count designed to produce a clear and glossy finish. The finished flat plate will be 10" (25.5 cm) in diameter by 1/2" (1.3 cm) thick.

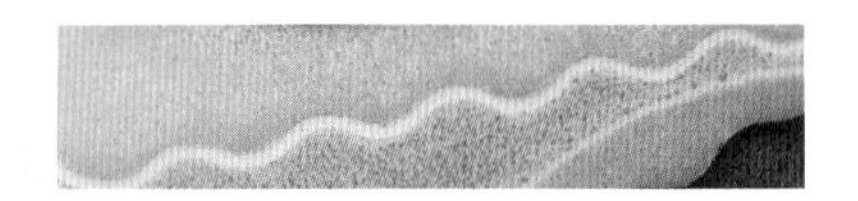

### *Tools & Equipment:*

- ***Kiln:*** Medium capacity fusing kiln with digital controller, kiln posts (assorted heights)
- ***Measuring & Setting:*** Weigh scale, small plastic bowls, measuring pitcher (with pour spout)
- ***Mold Preparation:*** Primo Primer™, applicator brush (soft, round), hairdryer
- ***Safety:*** Dust mask, safety glasses, kiln gloves

### *Materials:*

- ***Glass Supplies:*** All glass for this project must have the same COE
- Glass billet - 6" x 9" x 3/4" (15 x 23 x 2 cm), urobium pink transparent

### *Forming Mold:*

- 'Colour de Verre' 10" (25.5 cm) disc fuser mold
- Plate slumping mold 10" (25.5 cm) - optional
- Hydroperm - gypsum cement used to produce permeable plaster molds for casting
- RTV (Room Temperature Vulcanization) - a silicone molding compound

(Note: Hydroperm & RTV are available from most glass fusing supply centers)

## *How It's Done*

This project requires a number of shallow plaster forms that will be placed in the bottom of the 'Colour de Verre' 10" disc plate mold. I decided to arrange 9 simple flower designs in a circular pattern. These plaster forms are created by pouring a casting material called Hydroperm into a flexible silicone mold. So the first step for this project is to create the flexible silicone mold.

**1.** I used a cast glass flower that I already had in my collection of glass objects as the model to form the RTV flexible silicone mold as shown in the photo on the next page (3rd photo down). See ProTip below for more options on models & forms.

### *ProTip: Finding a Good Model*

The model I used here is one that I cast in glass several years ago, but the model does not have to be a cast glass form. It could be almost anything from a child's toy to a shape you make yourself from wax, clay or even plasticine. The only precaution is it must be shallow - no more than 3/8" (9.5 mm) thick and the sides should slant outward slightly (so the shape is wider at the bottom). Also try to avoid 'undercuts' within the design, these can prove to be problematic when you're removing the plaster form from the glass after casting.

2. Use a little glue to secure the model to the inside bottom of a small plastic bowl. Carefully read and follow the package directions on the RTV silicone molding compound. If required, coat the bowl and model with a release agent. Mix the RTV silicone, in your measuring pitcher (with pour spout) and pour it into the molding bowl to cover the model by at least 3/8" (1 cm) and allow it to cure (this could take from 1 hour to 24 hours, depending on the RTV product used). When the RTV is ready, pop it out of the plastic bowl then remove the model from the silicone mold to reveal the negative mold space.

3. The shallow plaster forms will be cast using Hydroperm casting cement (or a similar plaster casting material). This material is ideally suited for this 'floating within the glass' process because it does not require a coating of release primer and that means it can pickup and hold extremely fine details and maintain a very smooth surface. Be sure to wear a dust mask while measuring out 100 grams of Hydroperm to 50 grams of water (yes, you need to weigh these measurements) and stir them together in a plastic measuring pitcher with a pour spout (or a mixing bowl) until the mixture is the consistency of heavy cream. Carefully pour the mixture into the silicone 'negative mold' until the plaster is level with the top opening and let it set for about 30 minutes until hard (follow the plaster manufacturer's directions). When the first plaster form is cured, carefully pop it out of the RTV mold then mix another batch of Hydroperm and repeat the process until you have enough plaster forms for your design (mine used 9 flowers).

### *ProTip: RTV ASAP*

You could speed up the plaster forming process by creating additional RTV molds from the same (or similar) model or make an assortment of RTV molds using a variety of models to create a distinctive design for your billet cast plate.

You may be able to find ready-made RTV molds available to purchase. Ask your local glass fusing supplier for their recommendation.

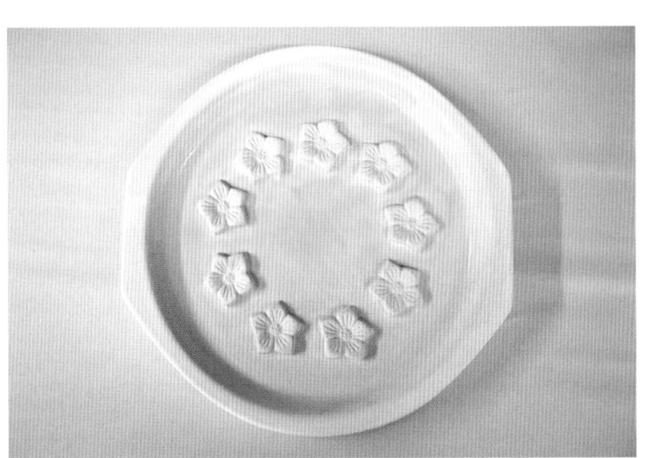

## *Billet Casting*

**1**. Next we'll secure the Hydroperm flowers to the floor of the disc fuser using a thick mixture of primer. Mix 1 part primer to 3 parts water and pour enough into the disc fuser to cover the bottom. This thick primer mixture will set up quickly so you won't have much time to arrange your plaster forms in the bottom of the disc mold.

**2**. I like to pick up the mold and move it around to distribute the primer mixture evenly. Be sure to cover both the floor and the inside wall of the mold. Now quickly (before the primer has a chance to set up) arrange your plaster forms on the mold floor to create your design.

**3**. Use a brush and the thick primer to fill in any spaces under the plaster forms. If these spaces are not filled the glass could flow under the plaster forms during the cast firing thereby trapping the Hydroperm flower inside the plate.

**4**. When the mold assembly is finished let the primer dry naturally, without using the hairdryer. Rapid dehydration by heating will cause this thicker primer to crack. Depending on humidity in your area the drying time could be anywhere from 12 to 24 hours.

**5**. When you are sure the mold is completely dry place it in the kiln. Lay three kiln posts on their side on the kiln shelf to elevate the mold during the firing then position the disc fuser mold on the kiln posts and check it for level and stability.

6. Clean your glass billet with a mixture of soap and water and dry it thoroughly with a soft towel. Carefully place it on top of the plaster flowers. Don't be concerned if the billet doesn't cover all the flowers, the glass is going to achieve full melt temperature and gravity will facilitate it to flow all around the flowers and fill the entire mold bottom.

| Firing Schedule for Casting the Billet Plate | | | | |
|---|---|---|---|---|
| Controller Segment | Ramp Rate (Per Hour) | Target Temperature | Heat Soak Hold Time | Interaction |
| Segment 1 | 150°F / 83°C | 200°F / 93°C | 4 Hours | None |
| Segment 2 | 150°F / 83°C | 1250°F / 675°C | 1 Hour | None |
| Segment 3 | 700°F / 389°C | 1440°F - 1460°F 782°C - 795°C | 35 to 45 minutes | Observe to Confirm Final |
| Segment 4 | AFAP - Down | 960°F / 515°C | 4 Hours | Do Not Vent |
| Segment 5 | 40°F / 22°C Ramp Down | 700°F / 370°C | 1 min | Do Not Vent |
| Segment 6 | 80°F / 44°C Ramp Down | 200°F / 93°C | 1 min | Kiln Off |
| Kiln off cool down - Do not vent - Cool to room temperature before opening | | | | |

7. They say that patience is a virtue and it may also be the most valuable characteristic to successfully complete this project. The casting billet that we're using for this project is very thick and the resulting cast plate is also very thick with the added complication of having several comparatively thinner areas where the plaster moldings are embedded. All this means that we need to be very patient and deliberate with this firing. We must ramp up slowly and soak often to prevent shocking the billet. When the firing arrives at full fuse temperature we'll have to wait for the molten glass to flow and form around the plaster moldings. On temperature down, a thick casting like this one requires adequate time to anneal soak and then finally it needs to be cooled in a very controlled and deliberate way. The result is a total kiln phase of almost 30 hours - plus the final cool down once the kiln has switched off (another 6 plus hours).

8. Be absolutely certain your casting is completely cool before opening the kiln to take it out. The last step is to remove the Hydroperm plaster from inside the glass. Do not submerge the fused plate in water while the Hydroperm forms are still in the glass. A water soak will cause the plaster to expand and will crack your glass. Thankfully, Hydroperm is relatively soft, simply break it out in small bits using a dental pick until each flower is cleaned. Then soak the finished plate in soap and water to remove any remaining fragments with a small scrub brush.

*The top photo shows the billet prior to firing, lower photo is the completed cast plate, after firing and cool down. The final step is to remove the Hydroperm plaster flowers from inside the glass.* *See the finished casting on page 66.*

# Chapter 11 - Pendants

## A Passion for Glass Jewelry

I have a passion for glass jewelry! My first 2 books, Innovative Adornments and Kiln Formed Bracelets were centered on glass jewelry. So it should come as no surprise that I have created mold designs for Color de Verre to make pendant castings. The projects presented in this chapter are small but powerful and make a wonderful fashion statement. The first pendant, 'Celtic Element,' will have the look of 'Pâte de Verre' with colorful details. The second pendant, 'English Floral,' will be cast using dichroic sheet glass to give it a shimmering finish.

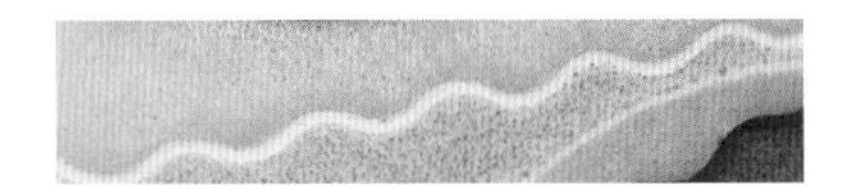

### Tools & Equipment:

- ***Kiln:*** Small 'table-top' fusing kiln with digital controller or Medium capacity fusing kiln with digital controller, kiln posts (assorted heights)
- ***Frit Measuring & Setting:*** Weigh scale, small plastic bowls, small funnel, plastic applicator bottle with fine tip, applicator spoons
- ***Mold Preparation:*** Primo Primer™, applicator brush (soft, round), hairdryer
- ***Safety:*** Dust mask, safety glasses, kiln gloves
- ***Glass Cutting and Shaping:*** Glasscutter, breaking pliers, diamond polishing pad, grinder with jewelry bit (optional)

### Materials:

- ***Adhesive:*** air dry adhesive (Bond 527 or E6000)
- ***Glass Supplies:*** All glass for this project must have the same COE

- Powdered Frit; sky blue, moss green
- Fine Frit; water clear
- Clear dichroic sheet - Thin (1.5 mm)
- Clear (or light pastel color) sheet glass - Std thick (3 mm)

### Forming Mold:

- 'Colour de Verre' Celtic Element Pendant Mold
- 'Colour de Verre' English Flower Pendant Mold

## 'Celtic Element' Pendant

1. Prepare the 'Celtic Element' pendant mold with primer. Remember to stir the primer mixture each time you dip your brush to keep it mixed well. Dry the mold between coats and after the final coat.

2. Use a plastic applicator bottle with a fine tip to fill the central design detail with moss powder frit and the outer design detail with sky blue powder frit.
3. Use a spoon to carefully backfill the pendant with 13 grams of water clear fine frit.
4. Lay some kiln posts on their side on the kiln shelf, place your filled mold in your kiln and close the lid. Fire the pendant using the firing schedule for 'Frit Cast Pendant.'

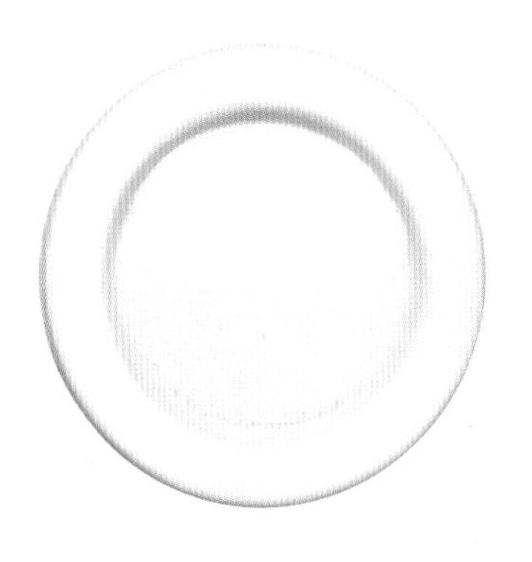

5. The final step is to fasten the casting to a commercially available sterling silver pendant frame (available from your local supplier). I used a length of silk cording in a complimentary color for the necklace I made. See photo below.

**Firing Schedule for Frit Cast Pendant**

| Controller Segment | Ramp Rate (Per Hour) | Target Temperature | Heat Soak Hold Time | Interaction |
|---|---|---|---|---|
| Segment 1 | 400°F / 222°C | 1410°F - 1420°F 765°C - 770°C | 10 to 15 minutes | Observe to Confirm Final |
| Segment 2 | AFAP Down | 960°F / 515°C | 30 min | Kiln Off |
| Kiln off cool down - Do not vent - Cool to room temperature before opening | | | | |

*This is the completed necklace mounted on a commercially available Sterling Silver pendant jewelry finding.*

*The cast pendant in the necklace above was created in a different mold, using the same technique.*

## 'English Floral' Pendant

1. Prepare the 'English Floral' pendant mold with primer as described in chapter 1 on page 8.
2. Cut a 1 1/2" (3.8 cm) square from a thin sheet of clear dichroic glass. Clean and place the glass with the coated dichroic side down against the mold.
3. Now cut another 1 1/2" (3.8 cm) square from a standard thick sheet of clear glass or light colored transparent glass. Clean and place this glass square on top of the dichroic glass. The pendant is now ready to be fired.
4. Lay kiln posts on their side on the kiln shelf, place your glass filled mold in your kiln and close the lid. Fire the pendant using the firing schedule for 'Sheet Cast Pendant.'
5. The finished cast dichroic pendant would look fabulous mounted on a sterling silver pendant frame (see page 7, middle right). Other possibilities would be to wire wrap it with gold or silver wire, or set it with a pendant bale. Discover many more ways to use these outstanding cast jewels in my first book 'Innovative Adornments.'

**Firing Schedule for Sheet Cast Pendant**

| Controller Segment | Ramp Rate (Per Hour) | Target Temperature | Heat Soak Hold Time | Interaction |
|---|---|---|---|---|
| Segment 1 | 400°F / 222°C | 1420°F - 1440°F<br>770°C - 782°C | 15 to 20 minutes | Observe to Confirm Final |
| Segment 2 | AFAP Down | 960°F / 515°C | 30 min | Kiln Off |
| Kiln off cool down - Do not vent - Cool to room temperature before opening | | | | |

# Chapter 12 - Kiln Formed Bracelets

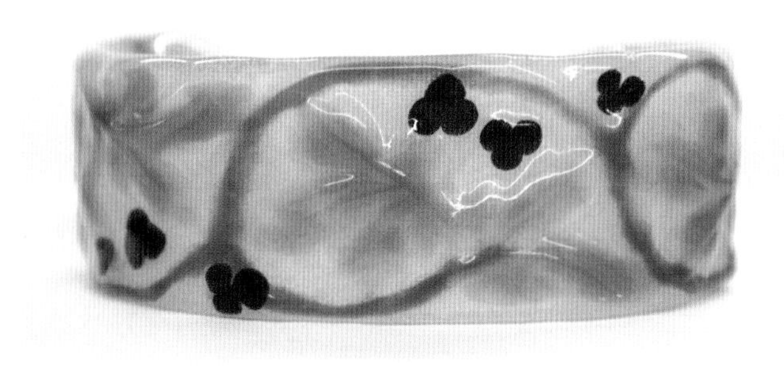

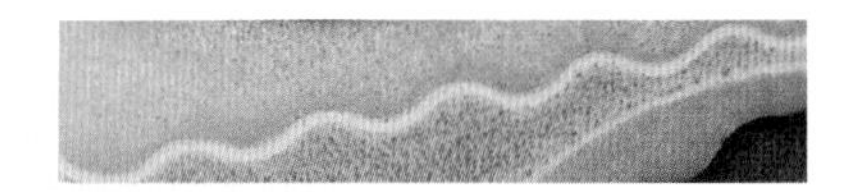

Kiln formed bracelets have been a prominent element in my glass career. Developing the process and designing the specialized tools for this technique was very gratifying. But the most rewarding aspect is teaching the process to thousands of fusers either at one of my personal workshops or through my book 'Kiln Formed Bracelets.' I truly feel this new book would not be complete without a chapter on bracelets.

I have designed several Colour de Verre molds to take advantage of the frit casting technique and my bracelet forming technique. I will feature two bracelets in this chapter, they are; Leaves and Berries and French Border. For the Leaves and Berries bracelet we will use the 'Pâte de Verre' coloring technique, filling in all the details with several colors of powder frit. The French Border bracelet will use a strip casting technique featuring dichroic sheet glass.

### Tools & Equipment:

- **Kiln:** Small 'table-top' fusing kiln with digital controller, kiln posts (assorted heights)
- **Frit Measuring & Setting:** Weigh scale, small plastic bowls, small funnel, plastic applicator bottle with fine tip, applicator spoons
- **Mold Preparation:** Primo Primer™, applicator brush (soft, round), hairdryer
- **Safety:** Dust mask, safety glasses, kiln gloves
- **Glass Cutting and Shaping:** Glasscutter, breaking pliers, glass grinder with standard bit, diamond polishing pad
- **Bracelet Forming Tools & Equipment:** bracelet forming mandrel, graphite forming tongs, fiber paper, hi-temperature Nichrome wire, minute timer, leather welding gloves
- **Bracelet Sizing Equipment:** steel ruler, marking pen, fabric measuring tape, digital calipers, sizing chart calculator (found in 'Kiln Formed Bracelets' book on pages 10 & 11)

### Materials:

- **Glass Supplies:** All glass for this project must have the same COE
- Powdered Frit; urobium pink, cherry red, moss green, dark green
- Clear dichroic sheet - Thin (1.5 mm)
- Pale gold transparent sheet - Std thick (3 mm)

### Forming Mold:

- 'Colour de Verre' French Border mold
- 'Colour de Verre' Leaves & Berries mold

## *Leaves and Berries*

1. Prepare the Leaves and Berries mold with primer as directed in chapter 1, pages 8 & 9. Dry with a hairdryer.
2. Use a plastic applicator bottle with a fine tip to place dark green powder frit in the vine detail. Change the color in the applicator bottle to moss green powder and fill the leaves sections. Finish the frit detail by filling the berries with cherry red powder.
3. Use a spoon to carefully backfill the mold cavity with 55 grams of urobium pink fine frit.
4. Lay a couple of posts on their side on the kiln shelf then place the bracelet mold assembly on these posts.
5. Close the lid and fire according to the firing schedule for 'Bracelet Frit Casting.'
6. When the bracelet blank is removed from the mold it shows the pattern with all the details that we are looking for. In the next few steps we will shape and custom size it.

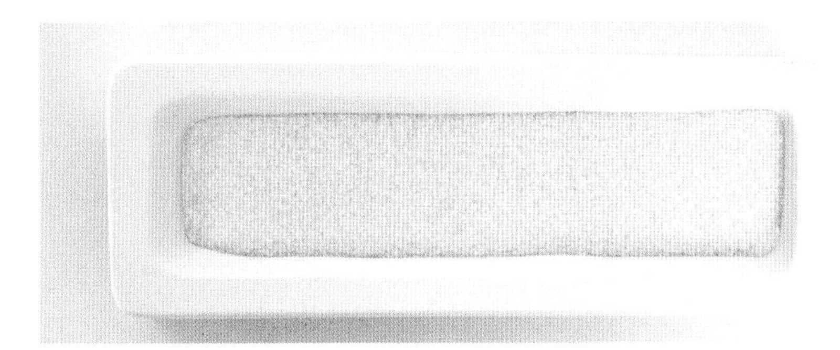

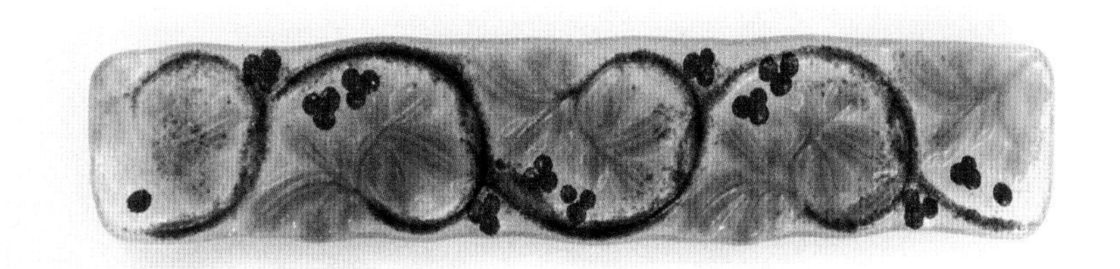

| Firing Schedule for Bracelet Frit Casting | | | | |
|---|---|---|---|---|
| Controller Segment | Ramp Rate (Per Hour) | Target Temperature | Heat Soak Hold Time | Interaction |
| Segment 1 | 400°F / 222°C | 1250°F / 675°C | 15 min | None |
| Segment 2 | AFAP - Up | 1410°F - 1420°F 765°C - 770°C | 15 to 20 minutes | Observe to Confirm Final |
| Segment 3 | AFAP Down | 960°F / 515°C | 1 hour | Kiln Off |
| Kiln off cool down - Do not vent - Cool to room temperature before opening | | | | |

## *Cold Working to Refine Bracelet*

**1**. Frit casting by its nature requires a little cold working to refine the ends and edges of the bracelet. In addition, the length of the bracelet blank must be determined and adjusted during this phase. Measure and carefully mark the blank length (see ProTip below left for more information) then use a glass grinder with a standard bit to adjust the length and round off the ends. You could also refine and shape the outer edge as I did for the bracelet shown in the photo below on this page.

**2**. After cold working (and sizing), the bracelet blank must be placed back into the casting mold to be fire polished. This will put a gloss on the edges that were dulled during cold working. Clean and dry the bracelet blank and remember to clean and re-coat the mold with fresh primer. Be careful to place the blank back into mold with the same orientation as it was originally cast, to match the molds' design details. Close the kiln and fire according to the schedule to 'Fire Polish a Bracelet Blank' below.

| **Firing Schedule to Fire Polish a Bracelet Blank** | | | | |
|---|---|---|---|---|
| Controller Segment | Ramp Rate (Per Hour) | Target Temperature | Heat Soak Hold Time | Interaction |
| Segment 1 | 400°F / 222°C | 1250°F - 1300°F<br>675°C - 705°C | 8 to 10 minutes | Observe to Confirm Final |
| Segment 2 | AFAP Down | 960°F / 515°C | 1 hour | Kiln Off |
| Kiln off cool down - Do not vent - Cool to room temperature before opening | | | | |

### *ProTip: Bracelet Sizing is Critical*

Anyone who has ever made one of these kiln formed bracelets knows that sizing is a critical step in the process. The length of the bracelet blank has to be custom sized to the wrist of the person who will eventually wear it. You can of course make a generic sized bracelet but the fit will not be as comfortable or as secure as a custom sized bracelet. The blank size must be set during the cold-working step. The custom measuring and sizing process is not difficult but it is too involved to reprint in this book. For clear instructions and details to properly size and kiln form one of these spectacular bracelets please refer to my book 'Kiln Formed Bracelets'.

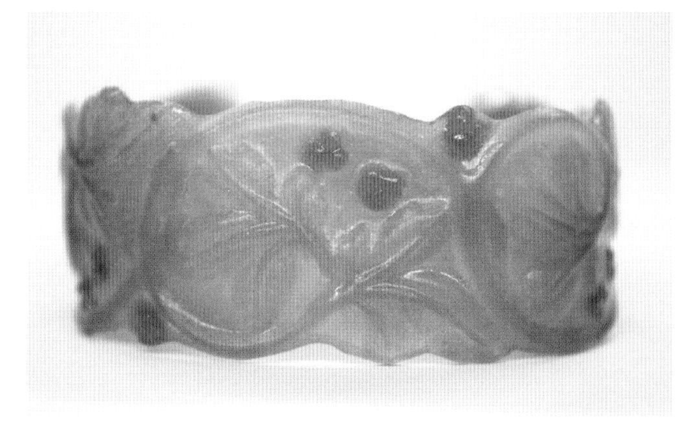

*The bracelet in this photo was cast in the same 'Leaves and Berries' mold as we used for this bracelet project. The frit color change certainly makes a very dramatic statement.*

## *Forming on the Bracelet Mandrel*

**Notice about these instructions:** The basic steps provided here are intended to serve as a refresher for crafters who have previous experience with bracelet kiln forming. If you have never completed a 'hot formed' bracelet on a mandrel, please do not attempt to do so by following the outline instructions presented here. For complete instructions to size and kiln form a bracelet - including the firing procedure, please refer to my book 'Kiln Formed Bracelets.'

1. After fire polishing, the blank is ready to be formed on the bracelet mandrel. This process is done in a small tabletop kiln. A frit cast bracelet has variable thicknesses therefore it must be heated and cooled slowly to prevent the glass from breaking.
2. Cover the bracelet mandrel with layers of fiber paper to custom size it (according to your measurements) and prevent the glass from sticking to the metal mold. This fiber paper is secured to the mandrel with Nichrome wire. Place the mandrel in the kiln then carefully position and balance the bracelet blank across the mandrel.
3. Turn the kin to the 'Low' setting for 8 minutes. Then turn the kiln up to the Medium setting until it has reached 900°F (482°C). You can now safely turn the kiln to the 'High' setting until it has reached the forming temperature range of somewhere between 1250°F to 1300°F (675°C to 705°C). It is ready to be shaped around the mandrel when the bracelet is fully slumped and softened. Note: This step is critical; be sure to review pages 18 to 21 in my book 'Kiln Formed Bracelets' for specific and detailed instructions.
4. Use graphite forming tongs to shape the bracelet around the mandrel. After the bracelet is formed it must be properly annealed (still on the mandrel) for 1 hour. The anneal soak time is determined by the blank's thickness, if in doubt always soak for a longer period rather than shorter. Over annealing will not hurt your piece but under annealing could be disastrous.

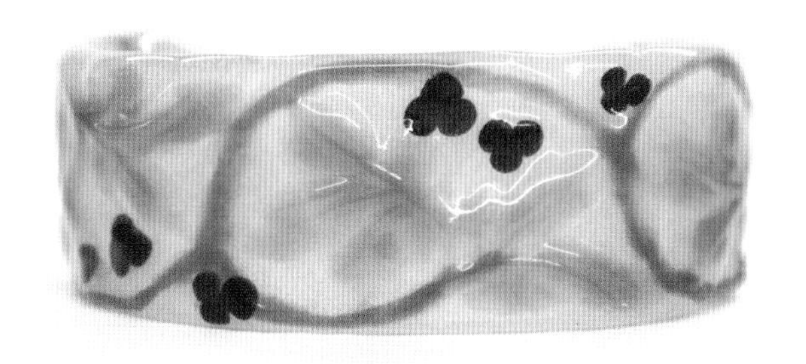

*Photo at right: The final 'Leaves and Berries' bracelet frit cast and kiln formed.*

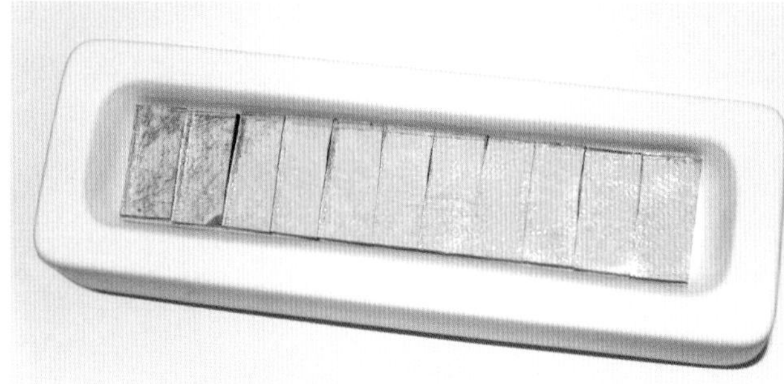

## Cast Dichroic Bracelet

1. Prepare the French Border mold with primer as directed in chapter 1 on pages 8 & 9 and dry it thoroughly with a hair dryer.
2. Cut a strip of clear dichroic glass 6 1/2" x 1 1/2" (16.5 x 3.8 cm). Clean and place this strip into the mold with the dichroic coated side down against the mold.
3. Cut a strip of pale yellow transparent glass 6 1/2" x 1 1/2" (16.5 x 3.8 cm) then divide and cut it into 9 or 10 sections. Cutting this strip into multiple sections will allow the air to escape during casting, keeping the occurrence of air bubbles in the bracelet to a minimum.
4. Clean and arrange these yellow sections (preferably in the same order as they were cut) in the mold, on top of the dichroic glass.
5. Place the assembly into your kiln by laying a couple of posts on their side on the kiln shelf then set the bracelet mold on these posts.
6. Close the kiln lid and fire according to the schedule for 'Cast Dichroic Bracelet.'
7. Remove the molded bracelet blank then refine the edges and size the blank as described in step 1 on page 76, also see ProTip bottom left on page 76.
8. After cold working place the blank back into the French Border mold for fire polishing, following step 2 on page 76.
9. Kiln form the bracelet as described on page 77.

**Firing Schedule for Cast Dichroic Bracelet**

| Controller Segment | Ramp Rate (Per Hour) | Target Temperature | Heat Soak Hold Time | Interaction |
|---|---|---|---|---|
| Segment 1 | 400°F / 222°C | 1250°F / 675°C | 20 min | None |
| Segment 2 | AFAP - Up | 1440°F - 1450°F 782°C - 788°C | 30 to 40 minutes | Observe to Confirm Final |
| Segment 3 | AFAP Down | 960°F / 515°C | 1 hour | Kiln Off |
| Kiln off cool down - Do not vent - Cool to room temperature before opening | | | | |

# Index